台灣傳統藝術之美

The Beauty of Traditional Arts in Taiwan

行政院文化建設委員會　指導
Directed by Council for Cultural Affairs, Executive Yuan

國立傳統藝術中心　策劃
Projected by National Center for Traditional Arts

遠流出版公司　執行
Edited and Produced by Yuan-Liou Publishing Co., Ltd.

台灣傳統藝術之美

The Beauty of Traditional Arts in Taiwan

• 廟會時，精采的陣頭吸引人群圍觀欣賞。
The spectacular parades always gather a crowd of audience in temple fairs.

● 皮影戲演師或坐或蹲，於幕後操弄戲偶。
The artists of Shadow Puppets, squatting or sitting,
manipulate the puppets in the back stage.

● 神韻動人的門神彩繪。
The appealing color painting of the Door Gods.

• 逛燈會，是傳統的元宵節活動。
Appreciating the lanterns is one of the traditional activities in the Lantern Festival.

Contents

目錄

絮根民間，立足國際

台灣的傳統藝術植根於生活中，與社會脈動相貼合，由在地人民的生活文化，發展出與其他國家相異的風格與情調，這是台灣最可貴的文化資產。

台灣各族群在長期的生活中，各自發展出精彩的文化藝術，在這塊土地上既有其獨特性，又互相影響；並在各時期吸收外來的各種元素，形成今日傳統藝術的面貌。在現代生活形態的衝擊下，屬於傳統農業社會脈絡中的傳統藝術，多面臨後繼無人、藝人凋零的困境。抽離了傳統生活的傳統藝術，如何在現代社會中找尋新的出路，是目前傳統藝術的重要課題。

對此，政府努力的方向，不只在於對過去的記錄與保存，或者辦理以傳統為名的活動；而更在於使傳統藝術能夠傳承並生根於民間，或者在傳統藝術轉型的過程中努力使其保有原來的傳統元素。簡單的說，為傳統藝術找回顧客，是使傳統藝術持續不墜的重要課題，這也是目前「文化創意產業」的重要精神。傳統藝術中深厚的文化內涵與智慧，貼近台灣生活的表現方式，更是文化創意產業的穩固根基。換言之，讓傳統藝術和現代的文化產業結合，是推動「文化創意產業」重要的一環。

《台灣傳統藝術之美》一書的出版，是在這種想法下的一個實踐；以現代的出版方式，來推廣傳統藝術，增加傳統藝術的認識人口。我們特別邀請在台灣傳統藝術領域深耕的專業研究者：鄭溪和、鄭昭民、陳怡方、趙綺芳撰文，同時並邀請在學術界研究多年的學者：汪志勇、呂錘寬、林會承、江韶瑩教授們審定。希望經由這本書所兼具的學術正確性與親切的推廣性，讓傳統藝術走出小眾。我們相信，傳統藝術不一定和商業機制的運轉相悖離，只要有適度的行銷與推廣，傳統藝術一樣可以在市場上佔有一席之地。

傳統藝術是台灣文化的具體展現。在全球化的浪潮下，如何在地球村中展現台灣存在的價值與特殊性？將台灣的傳統藝術推上國際舞台，是台灣在世界發聲的重要方式。這本書採用中英對照的方式，希望讓更多的國際友人看到台灣。

行政院文化建設委員會主任委員

From Indigenous Reinforcement to International Perspective

The traditional art of Taiwan is rooted deeply into daily life, and pulse synchronically with the society. Based on its way of life and culture, Taiwan has developed such a culture, delicate and exotic, extremely to the others. It is, indeed, the true heritage of Taiwan.

Under the impact of modern life style, the traditional art, derived from agricultural society, has been struggling for continuity, due to the lack of proper successors and the loss of elderly artists. How to break the ice and revive the traditional art, as it has lost its fertile ground, has been the most important consideration.

Whereas the plight, the government has taken action against the stranded situation, not just to record and preserve the past, or sponsor festivals in the name of promoting traditional issues, but to root it deep into everyday life again, or, while transforming, to maintain its classic elements. In short, it is a process to recruit the participators, performers and audiences, in order to sustain the traditional art, and this is the most essential spirit of the presently promoting concept of "cultural originality industry" is about. The profound significance and wisdom embedded in the traditional art, and the manifestation that is so close to the land and life will form a solid ground for the cultural originality industry. In other words, to promote the cultural originality industry, the integration of the traditional art and modern cultures is inevitable.

The issuing of *The Beauty of Traditional Arts in Taiwan* is the pleasant result of such an idea, and that is to take advantages of nowadays publishing methods to promote the traditional art, and to increase the participators. We have been assisted, encouragingly and gladly, by the knowledgeable scholars of various fields relating to the traditional art of Taiwan: Cheng Hsi-ho, Cheng Chao-min, Chen Yi-fang, Chao Chi-fang who wrote the articles; and intellectually accomplished professors, Wang Chi-yong, Lu Chui-kuan, Lin Huei-cheng, Chiang Shao-ying who examined and revised the publication.

We sincerely hope that the accuracy of knowledge and the cordiality within will help the promotion, and through proper marketing, the traditional art of Taiwan will become one of the best-sellers, in a conventional and culture sense.

The traditional art is a crystallized presentation of the Taiwanese culture. For better and more efficient expressing the value of Taiwan's existence and contribution in our global village, and to promote the traditional art in the brilliant international stage, we managed the bilingual edition, for sharing with our honorable friends around the world.

Minister, Council for Cultural Affairs,
Executive Yuan

● 作工精細的鑿花。
Painstakingly accomplished wood carving.

共賞傳統藝術之美

台灣的傳統藝術涵蓋許多面向，且各有其迷人的風貌，舉例言之：百看不厭的歌仔戲，鑼鼓喧天的北管樂，工法精緻的傳統彩繪，樸拙動人的竹編蒸籠，熱鬧的跳鼓陣等等。在眾多的種類中，《台灣傳統藝術之美》選取三十餘種傳統藝術來介紹，以精選的照片與細緻的編排，呈現各種傳統藝術的視覺之美。

《台灣傳統藝術之美》由國立傳統藝術中心策劃，遠流出版公司編輯製作。以往傳藝中心的出版大多著重於知識的保存與推廣；到目前為止，這是台灣第一本以平面圖像欣賞為主體，以美感的體驗來推廣傳統藝術的書。此次為使傳統藝術的推廣走上國際舞台，使國際友人認識台灣的傳統藝術，書中特別以中英對照的編排方式呈現，並且盡量以淺顯易懂，但又不失知識深度的文字，引導讀者穿透文化分殊性的隔離，體驗台灣最具特色的傳統藝術。

本書以六個主題來介紹台灣的傳統藝術，分別是：戲曲之美、音樂之美、建築工藝之美、民間工藝之美、舞蹈之美、陣頭技藝之美。每個主題先以一篇總論作為前導，介紹該類傳統藝術的內涵與概況，繼而以精彩的照片吸引讀者進入傳統藝術的氛圍。

因應各主題的特性，在各主題下再細分欣賞子題，例如，在「戲曲之美」的主題中，再分為歌仔戲、皮影戲、客家戲、傀儡戲、布袋戲等欣賞子題。每一個子題以一段說明文字為起始，讓讀者更具體認識該項傳統藝術的內涵；並隨即安排圖片的欣賞，輔以簡要的圖片說明，呈現傳統藝術兼具知性與感性的美感。

國立傳統藝術中心在今（九十二）年十月常態開園後，參觀遊客絡繹不絕，足見傳統藝術有其魅力與市場，未來亦可望吸引國際遊客參觀。期望這本書可以作為一種觸媒，引發國外遊客對台灣傳統藝術的興趣與一探究竟的動力；另一方面，本書也可讓遊客在遊園之後，細細品味豐富的傳統藝術之美。

國立傳統藝術中心主任

● 熱鬧喜氣的跳鼓陣。
Joyous and noisy Jumping Drum Array.

Sharing the Beauty of the Traditional Arts

The traditional arts of Taiwan cover tremendously great and multi-layered aspects, and each own its irreplaceable charms and glamour, to give a few examples, the cordial Taiwan Opera, the melodious Peikuan Music, the intricate traditional color-painting, the plain but affecting bamboo steamers, and the joyous Jumping Drum Array. Among the most representative arts, we have included more than thirty traditional artistic forms in this book to present the visual beauty of the traditional arts, by a delicate selection of photographs and careful editing.

The Beauty of Traditional Arts in Taiwan is projected by National Center for Traditional Arts, and edited by Yuan-Liou Publishing Company. National Center for Traditional Arts has issued great amount of publication that emphasized on the preservation and promotion of knowledge. So far, this is the first book in Taiwan, which uses images to inspire aesthetic sensibilities, and with the hope, to achieve further and deeper love of the traditional arts. This is a bilingual edition, both in Chinese and English, and with simple but accurate and in-depth captions, to walk the readers through the barrier of different cultures, and share the most distinctive traditional arts together.

The book included six parts: The Beauty of Opera, The Beauty of Music, The Beauty of Architecture, The Beauty of Folk Crafts, The Beauty of Dance and The Beauty of Folk Festival Parades. Each chapter proceeds with an introduction of the art form and profile, and is continued by deliberately selected photographs to accompany the reader into a virtual artistic world.

According to the features of the very theme, each is divided into several detailed subjects, for example, in The Beauty of Opera, it is categorized into Taiwan Opera, Shadow Puppet, Hakka Opera, String Puppet, Taiwan Glove Puppet and so on. Each subject is initiated by a brief introduction to help the reader with a better understanding of the traditional art; and what followed are the photographs and captions, and therefore, the presentation of knowledge and beauty is within.

After the grand opening in October, 2003, National Center for Traditional Arts has been a popular site to the visitors, and it reinforced the market and charms of the traditional art, and the attractions to foreign visitors is foreseen. We do hope this book will inspire people from different cultures and countries to explore the beautiful Taiwan's traditional arts, and will be the media for all of you to recollect the pleasant flavor of our traditional arts after visiting us.

Director, National Center for Traditional Arts   Ko Chi-Liang

• 台北保安宮的燈籠。
The lanterns in Pao An Temple, Taipei.

The Beauty of Opera

戲曲之美

戲曲之美

審定◎汪志勇　國立高雄師範大學國文系教授
撰文◎鄭溪和　國立高雄師範大學音樂系講師

十七世紀以後，大量的漢人從中國大陸來台灣拓墾，墾民以福建、廣東兩省最多。一九四九年隨政府來台的大陸軍民，則形成新的族群，加上最早居於本島的原住民，台灣人口結構呈現原住民、閩南、客家、外省（新住民）四大族群的局面。

原住民有極其豐富的音樂文化，但並未出現戲曲的表演藝術。而漢人社會中，戲曲早有完備的發展，並且與社會脈動、個人生命禮俗息息相關。舉凡民俗節慶、廟宇慶典、家族婚喪喜慶、民眾還願，甚至連私人污染環境、亂捕魚蝦等違規事件，都會被公部門「罰戲一檯」，可見戲曲與漢人社會生活之緊密關係。

離鄉背井來到台灣的漢人，將家鄉的傳統戲曲一起帶來是極自然之事，總計在台灣出現過的戲曲有——
大戲：歌仔戲、採茶戲、梨園戲、高甲戲、粵劇、亂彈戲、四平戲、閩劇、越劇、評劇、陝劇、豫劇、江淮劇、滇劇、湘劇、川劇、晉劇、崑劇、京戲、南管戲、北管戲。
小戲：車鼓戲、客家三腳採茶戲。
偶戲：傀儡戲、皮影戲、布袋戲。

其中梨園戲、高甲戲、亂彈戲、四平戲、車鼓戲、客家三腳採茶戲、傀儡戲、皮影戲、布袋戲、南管戲、北管戲，來台甚早。而歌仔戲則是台灣先民共同的傑作，這些戲曲與早期台灣社會有較為緊密的關係，其餘劇種來台時間多為一九四九年以後。

戲曲的表演是以樂曲搬演故事，表演時，演員必須擁有一身唱、唸、做、打的良好基本功。所謂「唱」，指的當然是演出時歌唱的部分；「唸」是台詞；「做」是肢體動作；「打」則是武打的招術。

傳統戲曲透過「虛擬象徵」的美學手法，將劇中情境展現出來。運用誇張、美化的肢體語言，表現喜、怒、哀、樂等情緒，這是「虛擬」的表現；而角色的分工、演員的化妝、服裝、道具、音樂、說白都使用「象徵」的手段。它與西方歌劇、話劇的寫實風格有著根本的不同。

一九六〇年代中後期，台灣逐漸轉型為工商社會，鄉村人口外流，致使傳統農村結構崩解，而屬於傳統社會的戲曲文化因此受到空前的衝擊，無以為繼，一一凋零，僅有京戲、豫劇因為受到政府資源的支持而有良好的發展。

一九八〇年代起，政府開始投注心力搶救傳統戲曲，獲得許多寶貴的資料與紀錄，但老藝人的凋零、欣賞人口的萎縮，仍是其發展的隱憂。幸而，至今有部分戲曲，如歌仔戲、布袋戲等，尚能因應現代社會轉型，出現更為精緻的表演模式，在現代劇場中擁有一席之地，顯示其強韌的生命力不容忽視。

聚精會神看戲的戲迷。
The concentrated lovers of Taiwan Opera.

The Beauty of Opera

Supervision: Wang Chi-yong   Professor, Chinese Department, National Kaohsiung Normal University

Text: Cheng Hsi-ho   Instructor, Department of Music, National Kaohsiung Normal University

Since 17th century, there were tremendous amount of Han settlers migrating to Taiwan, and among them, the Fukien and the Cantonese exceeded that from other provinces in numbers. What is more, there were Mainland soldiers and civilian, conducted by the government, moved to Taiwan, and formed a new component to the big family, and made the structure of Taiwanese population quartered by the Aboriginal peoples, Fukien, Hakka and other provinces (New Residents).

The musical heritages of the Aboriginal peoples are extremely rich, however, there was no opera performing art developed. On the contrary, the Han (Fukien, Hakka and New Residents) society has a long history of traditional operas of their own, that are intimately connected to their social and personal aspects; and the coverage is wide that not just folk customs and ceremonies, temple fairs, family wedding and funerals, as well as redeem a vow to gods are included, even pollution caused by the individuals, illegal fishing and etc. would be requested to hire a opera troupe to perform as a penalty. The closeness between opera and Han's daily life is clearly explicated.

For those Hans who were away from their own roots, it was normal that they brought their traditional operas with them to their settlements. Examining the history, there were:

The Grand Operas: Taiwan Opera, Hakka Tea-picking Opera, Theater Opera, Kao Chia Opera, Cantonese Opera, Luan-tan Opera, Siping Opera, Fukien Opera, Shaosing Opera, Ping-ju Opera, San Opera, Honan Operaa, Jian Huai Opera, Yunnan Opera, Hunan Opera, Sichuan Opera, Shan-si Opera, Kiangsu Kunshan Opera, Peking Opera, Nankuan Opera and Peikuan Opera.

The Mimic Opera: Che Gu Opera (Cart Drum Opera), Hakka Three-performer Tea-picking Opera.

The Puppet Show: String Puppet Show, Shadow Play, Taiwan Glove puppet Show.

Among these, Theater Opera, Kao Chia Opera, Luan-tan Opera, Siping Opera, Che Gu Opera, Hakka Three-per-former Tea-picking Opera, String Puppet Show, Sahdow Play, Taiwan Glove-puppet Show, Nankuan Opera and Peikuan Opera arrived Taiwan much earlier than the rest. Taiwan Opera is a marvelous form developed by earlier settlers, and was very intimate to the society of Taiwan of the time. The rest of the forms were brought in by the New Residents by 1949.

A traditional opera is to perform the story by using music, and to be an excellent performer, he must be good, at the same time, at singing, reciting and being neat in body language and martial art.

The traditional operas, through aesthetic fictional symbols, express the scenes. And, for reinforcement, exaggerating and beautified body language was applied to present cheerfulness, anger, sadness and joyousness. This is a fictional presentation; and the cast of characters, make up, wardrobe, stage props, music and narrations are all symbolic. It has fundamentally different to the realistic Western opera.

During mid- and late 60s, Taiwan transferred to an industrial and commercial society, the rate of outward migration rose ever higher, and the traditional rural structure collapsed, accordingly, the operas belonging to the traditional society confronted unprecedented impact. Most of them failed to survive, and only Peking and Honan operas continued, due to the strategic protections from the government.

Since 1980s, the government awakened to the importance of rescuing and preserving traditional operas, and thus tremendous amount of information and documents were restored. However, with the loss of elder performers and the reduction of the audiences, the revival developed is overshadowed. Fortunately, there are some performing forms, such as Taiwan Opera, Taiwan Glove Puppet Show have answered to the transformation of the modern society, and developed much intricate performing style, thus, possessed a strong standing ground. Their intense vitality is somehow overwhelming.

• 歌仔戲的武打場面，帶動整場觀眾熱烈的氣氛。
The martial scene of Taiwan Opera is a catalyst to the audience's enthusiastic mood.

歌仔戲

歌仔戲在二十世紀初期左右誕生於台灣，是唯一土生土長的戲曲。由於表演元素如語言、音樂等，取材於當地，因此一推出即受到民眾熱烈的喜愛。台灣社會的變動使得許多劇種因此消失或式微，但歌仔戲卻仍活躍至今；藝人大多能隨順自然的適時調整，展現出草根性的強韌生命力。多變的面貌，一直是歌仔戲的現象，也是其傳統。

TAIWAN OPERA

Taiwan Opera came to solid existence in the early 20th century, and is the only locally born and bred opera. Due to the essential elements, such as language, music and etc., were obtained locally, it was much appreciated once staged. The rapid social change in Taiwan withered very many operas, however, Taiwan Opera lasts vigorously, and the performers are able to the transition properly, and both show the ingenious and vital regionalism. Being diverse is one of outstanding characteristics of Taiwan Opera, and an unchangeable tradition.

- 「本地歌仔」是歌仔戲的雛形，也是早期人民農閒時的重要娛樂。目前在宜蘭羅東公園仍經常聚集一群喜愛歌仔的民眾，以樂會友，自得其樂。（圖 1,3）
  Local songs is the model of Taiwan Opera, and an important recreation in earlier agricultural society; even nowadays, there are still lovers of local songs gathering in Luodong Park, Yilan, to sing and entertain each other. (photos 1, 3)

- 本地歌仔的主要伴奏樂器為殼子弦（圖3右二演奏者）與大廣弦（圖2右演奏者）；雖然不是歌仔最主要的樂器，但音色蒼涼獨特，是台灣獨有的絃樂器。
  Ke zai string (photo 3, second from right, performing) and da guang string (photo 2, right, performing) are the major musical instruments for local songs. Though not the major instruments to Taiwan Opera, their sophisticated and melancholy tones are unique to Taiwan.

● 苦旦悲情的演技，最能搏得觀眾的同情。
圖為《尪某情》的小旦演出。
The sorrowful female character usually
gains tremendous sympathy. The photo
shows "dan" the female lead's performance.

● 扮相俊美的小生是目光的焦點，通常也是劇團負責人。
圖為《尪某情》的小生扮相。
With handsome stage appearance, "sheng" (the male
lead) is often the focus of the drama, and usually is the
manager of the troupe. The photo shows the sheng in
the drama "Love of the Wife and Husband".

- 廟宇慶典時聘請劇團演出的扮仙戲，是為神明而演出，在正式開演前表演。（圖1）
  Fairy Presentation is essential in temple fairs, and is a performance for gods. It performs before main performance. (photo 1)

- 傳統歌仔戲的戲目有歷史戲與胡撇仔戲之分。歷史戲是傳統劇目，胡撇仔戲則是現代新編劇。圖為著名歷史戲《白蛇傳》的主角，許仙（圖2）、白蛇（圖3）與青蛇（圖4）。
  Traditional Taiwan Opera programs are categorized into historical drama and "hu pie" drama. The historical dramas are conventional, while hu pie dramas are modern new productions. The photo shows the famous historical "The Legend of the White Snake" and its major leads, Shu Sian (photo 2), White Snake (photo 3) and Green Snake (photo 4).

- 現代歌仔戲團常自行創作新的演出腳本，主題多樣，並精心設計新造型，扮相華麗。（右圖）
  Modern Taiwan Opera troupes usually create their own new productions. The themes vary, and character modeling ingenious, and the appearances are especially shining. (photo, right)

- 歌仔戲的劇本常安排許多悲苦的情境，來增加戲劇的衝突點，並配合演員所唱的〈哭調〉，營造出令觀眾感動不已的氛圍。（圖1,4）
  It is very often that the scripts of Taiwan Opera are related to sad stories, in order to increase the conflicts. It is performed with "crying tones", and push the very sad scenarios to a sad and touch climax.(photos 1, 4)

- 武打場面讓戲的節奏富於變化，打鬥中各色大旗的出現，代表水、火、風等的侵襲，身陷其中的演員必須以武功克服險境。（圖2）
  Martial art scenarios are full of rhythmic changes. While fighting, there are large flags flapping on stage, representing the violent water, fierce fire and bleak wind, and it is usually a scene to show how the protagonist overcome a dangerous situation. (photo 2)

- 幻想式的《唐明皇遊月宮》一劇，劇情節奏起伏，頗能擄獲觀眾的心。（圖3）
  Imaginative "The Travel of Tan Ming Huang to the Moon Palace" has very creative and undulating plots that keep the audiences' hearts so charmingly captured. (photo 3)

- 狹小的後台是演員上粧的地方，五顏六色的彩筆恣意在臉上揮灑。沒一會兒功夫，生、旦、淨、丑的角色將一一呈現在觀眾面前。（圖1-4）

The narrow back stage is where the performers do their make up. Just in a very short moment of work, the colors turn them into male lead (sheng), female lead (dan), painted-faced character with strong personalities (Jing), comic or villain character (chou) suddenly come to life in front of the audiences. (photos 1-4)

- 後台也是撫育小孩的場所。戲班成長的孩子，少不了在後台玩耍的童年經驗。（圖5）

The back stages are a place to take care of performer's children. Whoever grows up in a troupe will not remember life without the memories of all the childhood fun there. (photo 5)

皮影戲

皮影戲是以獸皮雕成人物剪影，利用燈光的照射，由演師於白色布幕後方操縱戲偶，並演唱曲調來敘述故事情節的偶戲。皮影戲大都在寺廟慶典或民眾酬神時演出，農曆七、八月是演出的旺季。在戶外的野台戲只能於晚間進行，才能演出影子的效果。一台戲約需四到七名人手，由一人主演、一人助演，其他則擔任後場樂器的演奏。

SHADOW PLAY

The leather silhouettes made out of animal skin are the leads in the Shadow Play. The operation is to projecting lights on the silhouettes from the back of a white screen, while the master artists manipulating the puppets, and singing and narrating for the puppets. Shadow Play only perform in temple fairs or when believers rewarding the gods for ex voto purposes, and the performing reaches its high peak around lunar July and August. When performing outdoors, it is only held during the night to avoid daylight. A Shadow Play is run by four to seven people; one of them as the leading artist, and one as his assistant, while the rest take charge of musical performing and other back stage trivialities.

- 為了讓肢體的各個部分靈活動作，皮影戲偶的頭、身、四肢是分別做好，然後組合而成。無言的戲偶等待演師的巧手梳理，準備上台戲弄一番。（圖1,2）
  To make the parts nimble, the head, body and limbs of a shadow puppet are made separately and assemble together with skills. Photo 1 and 2 show the silent puppet are taken care by the artist for a glorious show ahead. (photos 1, 2)

- 偶頭是展現人物性格的重要部位，由於演出時戲偶必須緊貼於布幕上，因此戲偶皆採側面雕刻。（圖3）
  The head is that shows the personality of a puppet. As the leather puppets must attached to the screen to create shadows, their profiles are intricately carved. (photo 3)

 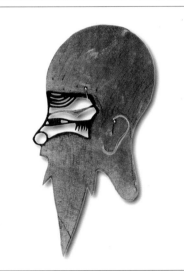 

● 在演師的巧手下，戲偶在光影的幻境中上演悲歡離合。
Through the skillful hands of the artist, the puppets emit implausible affections in the dreamland-like stage.

• 各式各樣的戲偶表現不同的故事情節。一尊皮影戲偶的誕生程序繁複,從
選皮、製皮、過稿、鏤刻、敷彩、曝曬、綴結到裝桿,才得以完成。
Each puppet are made for different stories. The process of making can be
complicated, from selecting cowhide, processing it into leather, carving, col-
oring, drying, connecting the parts, and finally, installing holding sticks
as completion.

傀儡戲

傀儡戲的歷史久遠，它與中國古代葬禮中用以殉葬的「俑」有直接的關係。歷代出現了各種不同類型的傀儡戲，如：懸絲傀儡、水傀儡、杖頭傀儡等等。台灣的傀儡屬於懸絲傀儡，戲偶身上綁著許多線，演師於幕後操作，讓戲偶做出肢體動作。傀儡戲是婚嫁、壽誕、嬰兒周歲、新居落成，甚至水災、火災、驅邪、除疫經常選用的戲種。

STRING PUPPET SHOW

String Puppet performance has a long history. It is directly related to the interred figures buried with the dead in ancient China. There are different types of string puppets in each the history, such as hanging string puppets, water puppets (performed in water), and stick puppets (performed with the support of sticks from below). Taiwan puppets are string puppets that hung on several strings in each key joints and manipulated to imitate real human movements by the artists in the back stage. String Puppet Show are often seen in weddings, birthday and infants' first anniversary of birth and when a new house is completed, as well as a way to drive away the evil force after catastrophic flood, fire and so on.

- 演師藏身幕後，牽動絲線操縱戲偶肢體動作，配合口白、唱腔表現劇中人物之性格。傀儡戲偶隨絲動作，身不由己，因此一般人常謔稱遭受控制的人為「傀儡」。（圖1-2）
  The artist, hiding behind the screen, controls the strings to manipulate the puppets, while singing and narrating for the puppets at the same time. As puppets are lifeless without the strings operated, people who can not do as they really wish are called puppets.(photos 1-2)

- 台灣傀儡戲偶的戲服刺繡精細，是傳統工藝的的最佳表現。（圖3）
  The wardrobe of the puppets are deliberately embroidered, and is one of the best presentations of the traditional craftsmanship. (photo 3)

客家採茶戲

流行於台灣北部客家聚落的客家採茶戲，以客家山歌、小調的基礎，發展出大戲形式的「採茶大戲」及小戲形式的「三腳採茶」。前者是一九一八年之後，受京戲、亂彈戲、四平戲影響而誕生，內容除傳統的歷史故事之外，也有許多客家的民間故事。後者則由一丑、二旦以對唱的表演為主，演出以「張三郎賣茶」為主題的劇目。

HAKKA TEA-PICKING OPERA

Popular in the Hakka communities in Northern Taiwan, Hakka Tea-picking Opera is based on Hakka folk songs and ditties. It is also the foundation of the Grand Tea-picking Opera and the Mimic Three-character Tea-picking Opera. The former was giving birth after 1918, being deeply influenced by Peking Opera and Luan-tan Opera, demonstrating historical stories, and also various Hakka folklores. And the latter is performed by one chou, the comic male character, and two dan, the female leads. With antiphonal singing as their major performing style, drama such as Chang San Lang Selling Tea and the others are presented.

- 客家採茶戲是源自客家人生活中的採茶工作，為日常生活轉化成表演藝術的著例。其中男女逗趣的場面是常見的主題。（圖1-3）
Hakka Picking-tea Opera is derived from daily tea picking work, and is one of the typical example demonstrating how daily life routine transferred to performing art. Teasing and making fun of each other is often seen in the opera. (photos 1-3)

● 採茶戲中婦女的典型裝扮——樸素的斗笠、放置茶葉的竹簍。
The costumes of characters are typical tea picking work dress, including simple leaf hats, bamboo baskets for keeping tea leaves.

• 圖中的男性皆為採茶戲的故事主角張三郎，以故事情節分為《糶酒》（圖
1）、《上山採茶》、《送郎十里亭》（圖2,3）、《桃花過渡》等。
The male performer in the photos is the protagonist of Chang San Lang
Selling Tea, and the dramas are titled according to the plots, such as Sell-
ing Wine (photo 1), Picking Tea Leaves in the Mountains, Accompanying
Her Lover to Shi-li Pavilion (photos 2, 3) and Tao-hua Crossing the Ferry.

南管戲與北管戲

台灣的南管戲主要是指梨園戲與高甲戲。梨園戲演唱南管音樂，唸白以福建泉州腔為標準，文白並用，表演風格細緻、典雅；高甲戲簡化南管音樂，填詞演唱，並加入北管鑼鼓以壯聲勢，故有「南唱北打」之稱。北管戲又稱為亂彈戲、外江戲，目前仍流傳下來的劇目約兩百齣左右，雖傳自大陸，但目前僅台灣保有此一劇種。

NANKUAN OPERA AND PEIKUAN OPERA

Nankuan Opera specifically indicates Theater Opera and Kao Chia Opera. Theater Opera performs Nankuan music, but the narration is typically Fukien Chuan Zhou tune that combines ancient Chinese literary language and Chinese vernacular. The performance style is intricate and elegant. Kao Chia Opera simplified Nankuan music, and adds lyrics to it. It is reinforced by Peikuan gongs and drums for magnificent momentum, and achieved the reputation of sining in Southern tune, but accompanied by Northern music. Peikuan Opera is also called Luan-Tan Opera, Wai Jiang Opera, and to this date, there are still two hundred dramas well preserved. It was originated in the China, but only survives in Taiwan.

- 唱腔高亢、武戲見長的北管戲，是過去廟宇慶典野台戲的大宗，目前多被歌仔戲取代。像宜蘭的福蘭社這樣，尚能演出的業餘子弟劇團實屬難得。（圖1-3）
With resounding tunes and excellent martial performance, Peikuan Opera was the major performing troupes in temple fairs. However, it has been largely replaced by Taiwan Opera, and there are only a few amateurs artists are able to perform full drama, such as the members of Fu Lan Troupe in Yilan. (photos 1-3)

• 曾是清代台灣主要劇種的南管戲，以細緻的文戲演出為特色。新錦珠劇團演出的《高文舉》，表現傳統劇目中經常出現的主題，描述男人飛黃騰達後拋棄糟糠之妻的情節。（圖1-4）

Nankuan was one of the major drama genre in the Ching Dynasty, and is famous for its delicate artistically non-martial performance. Kao Wen Ju, performed by Shing Jin Zhu Troupe, is one of the dramas frequently presented, that depicting how a now glorious man deserted his wife who once shared all his hard lot. (photos 1-4)

布袋戲

清代時，布袋戲從福建傳至台灣，初期完全繼承閩南布袋戲的傳統，以文戲為主，風格悠雅、細緻，節奏緩慢。其後，藝人改用台灣北管的戲曲、戲文，武戲增加，節奏緊湊。一九六〇年代以後，金光布袋戲出現，舞台不再雕樑畫棟，戲偶加大，配樂以唱片取代傳統後場，並逐漸發展出聲光效果強大的霹靂系列，在台灣擁有廣大的觀眾群。

TAIWAN GLOVE PUPPET

Glove puppet performance handed down to Taiwan during the Ching Dynasty, and in early days, it inherited fully the traditions of Fukien Glove Puppet presentations, focused on non-martial drama, with elegant and intricate style and slow tempo. After the 1960s, Jian Kuang (electrical and with special effects) Glove Puppets troupes emerged from conventional scene. The stages were no longer classically carved with intricate patterns, but replaced by moveable background, and the size of the puppets were enlarged. What is more, there's no more on-site accompanying musicians, but substituted with records. Later, Pi Li (thunderbolt) series, with intensive light and sound effects were developed and now passionately embraced by the audiences.

● 野台布袋戲以耀眼的色彩彩繪戲台，在紛雜的空間中爭取觀眾的注目。結合中西流行音樂的音響取代了傳統的後場，成為今天主要的配樂方式。（右圖）
The stages of outdoor Glove Puppets are colorfully painted, in order to attract the audiences, and popular music has replaced traditional back stage music performing, and promoted itself as the major incidental music. (photo, right)

• 精緻典雅的雕工與服飾，使嬌小的古典布袋戲偶本身即令人目不轉睛；加上演師細膩的指上工夫，戲偶宛如真人般生動。
Deliborate and classic carving and costumes make those small puppets extremely eye-catching, and the skillful manipulation gives life to the puppets as if they are real people.

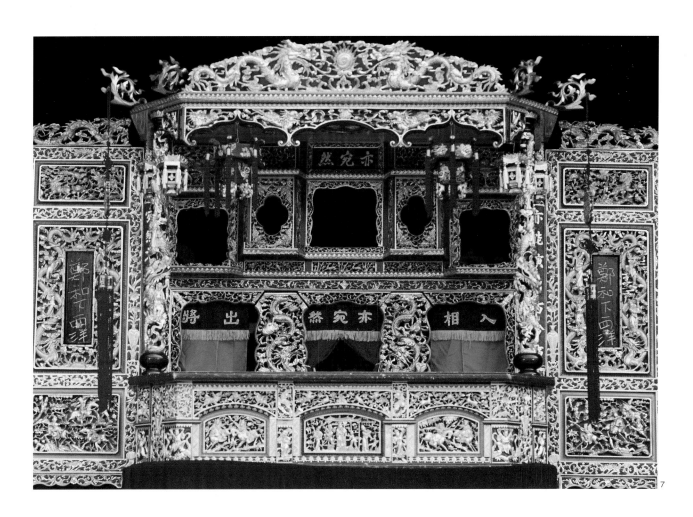

7

• 古典布袋戲台講究木刻雕工，精細的配件彷彿真實傳統建築之縮影。
金色與紅色為主調的搭配，展現富麗堂皇的氣派。（圖1-7）
The stage of classic Glove Puppets Show are very fastidious about
wood carving, and the exquisite components look like exact miniatures
of authentic traditional buildings. Gold and red are two major colors
used to express the magnificent air. (photos 1-7)

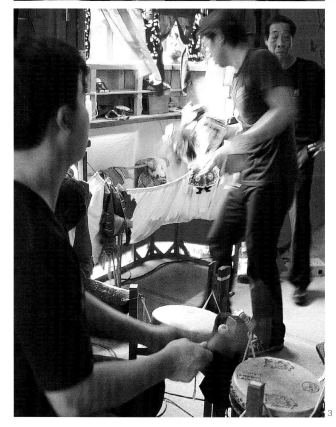

• 前台演師與後台伴奏的樂師們賣力演出，讓台下的觀眾目不轉睛的隨著戲偶或喜或憂。（圖 1,3,4）
The performing artists and back stage artists worked together deliberately and caused the audiences so concentrated on the puppets performing and even drawn by the protagonists emotionally. (photos 1, 3, 4)

• 古典布袋戲的後場是由樂師現場伴奏，鑼鼓與嗩吶常用於熱鬧的武戲演出。（圖 2）
The classic Glove Puppet Show is accompanied with on-site musicians' performing, and the gongs, drums, and suona horns (Chinese trumpets) increased the power of warfare scene. (photo 2)

• 口白（台語）：「金光閃閃，瑞氣千條。萬惡的罪魁走哪裡去！」
Line (in Taiwanese): Glistening the golden lightning glistening, cover-
ing the air auspicious force, the most vicious villain fail to escape!

- 洞房花燭夜與金榜題名時是傳統社會對人生幸福的期待，布袋戲演出結尾時，常會擺出「尪某對」象徵圓滿結局，也祝福觀眾。（上圖）
Getting married and becoming a high-rank official were what one would regard as the supreme expectations of life, so that a Glove Puppet Show are conventionally ends with "husband and wife's reunion", as a symbol of happy ending, and also to give best wishes the audience.

- 布袋戲的角色有：白淨的「文生」（圖1,6,9）、武功高強的「武生」（圖2）、甘草人物的「笑」（圖3）、年輕女性的「旦」（圖4）、沉穩智慧的「老生」（圖5）、性情暴烈的「花臉」（圖7,8）。
The characters are grouped into fair wen sheng (elegant young male lead, photos 1, 6, 9), highly martial wu sheng (martial male lead, photo 2), funny and comic siao (pantaloon, photo 3), gentle and beautiful dan (young female lead, photo 4), stable and experienced lao sheng (older male lead, photo 5) and fiery-tempered hua lian (painted-faced character with strong personalities, photos 7, 8).

● 霹靂布袋戲的巨型戲偶與偶像酷炫的造型，加上電影般的拍攝手法，吸引許多年輕人熱中扮演戲中角色。
Giant puppiets of Pi Li Glove Puppet are gorgeously designed, and the show is often shot with motion picture techniques that intrigues very many young people to mimic the chracters.

The Beauty of Music

音樂之美

音樂之美

審定◎呂錘寬　國立台灣師範大學民族音樂研究所教授
撰文◎鄭溪和　國立高雄師範大學音樂系講師

台灣傳統音樂是由原住民音樂、客家音樂、南管音樂、北管音樂、戲曲音樂等，共同組合而成豐富、多樣的音樂版圖。其中原住民音樂是唯一非屬漢族系統的音樂，其音樂少有器樂的發展，然而歌樂方面卻有著從最簡單到最複雜的歌唱方式，敘述與生活息息相關的各項主題。

南管音樂與北管音樂是台灣漢族傳統音樂的主軸，涵蓋的層面最為廣泛。南管音樂擁有悠久的歷史，至今仍保有古風，有「音樂活化石」之稱。狹義的南管音樂專指南管而言，樂風典雅肅穆，以其特有的譜式── 南管譜記寫樂章。曲目依其特徵分有指、譜、曲三類，形式嚴謹。廣義的南管音樂，除了南管之外，尚有品管、太平歌、車鼓、南管戲唱腔、高甲戲唱腔等，樂風相較於南管則顯得活潑而通俗。

北管音樂樂風粗獷、典雅兼而有之，但以粗獷豪邁較為人知悉，使用流傳較廣的工尺譜記譜。曲目可分為鼓吹樂、絲竹樂與細曲。每當廟宇神誕時，北管音樂總是隊伍中最引人注目的音樂團體，由於樂隊編制不若南管嚴格，且隨機性高，在許多傳統音樂系統中，都可以看到北管的影子。

客家音樂有歌樂與器樂兩類，歌樂方面為客家山歌，器樂則為八音。客家山歌是該族群耕種、採茶、勞動而產生的歌曲，台灣南北兩地各有不同的曲目。八音有鼓吹及絃索兩種形式，活躍於客家村落之歲時祭儀、生命禮俗、廟會慶典等活動。

布農族的八部合音宛如天籟。
Bunun tribe's eight-part chorus is as beautiful as heavenly songs.

台灣擁有多樣的傳統戲曲。傳統戲曲的表演，是「前場」的演員和「後場」的音樂，共同組合而成；「後場」即是戲曲音樂。台灣各劇種使用的音樂，大致有南管、北管、歌仔、客家等音樂系統。傳統上，一齣戲曲的音樂組成，是運用現有的音樂進行「組合」或「變奏」，不同於西方歌劇的作曲家是配合劇情創作歌曲。「組合」不同的曲子來貫穿全劇的手法，稱為「曲牌體」，如南管、歌仔系統；而將曲子依情節、角色的需要進行「變奏」的，則稱為「板腔體」，如北管系統。

台灣傳統音樂長久以來深植民間，擁有大量的經典曲目。可惜在過去的音樂教育體系中受到忽視，一般大眾雖經多年學校教育課程，仍對身旁的音樂毫無所悉。隨著藝人凋零、技藝失傳，欣賞人口也跟著大量流失，台灣傳統音樂正面臨極大考驗。值此時刻，傳統音樂的傳承與發揚工作更顯其重要性。

The Beauty of Music

Supervision: Lu Chui-kuan   Professor, Graduate Institute of Ethnomusicology, National Taiwan Normal University

Text: Cheng Hsi-ho   Instructor, Department of Music, National Kaohsiung Normal University

The traditional music of Taiwan extensively includes music of Aboriginal peoples, Hakka, Nankuan, Peikuan and various local operas, and forms a rich and diverse music domain. As the only non-Han and almost exclusively vocal, the music of the Aboriginal peoples, though almost with substantial instrumental development, is outstanding for its ability to properly express no matter simple daily life or complicated rituals.

Nankuan and Peikuan are still the mainstream of traditional music in Taiwan. Nankuan has a long developing history, and continues to maintain its archaism, thus, it is reputably called the living fossil of music. In a narrower sense, Nankuan only indicates the Nankuan music itself. The elegant and solemn Nankuan are written in its own special notations. According to its nature, the notations are categorized into three groups, with very exact forms: suite, single songs and program music.

From a larger angle, Nankuan also covers Pinkuan, Taipin Songs. Chegu, Nankuang tunes and Kaujia tunes, and in general, their styles are much lighter and popular than Peikuan itself.

Though both unconstrained and classic, Peikuan is more known as heroic intrepid and epic. Gongchepu (the Chinese solfege notation) is used by Peikuan, and the tunes are categorized into trumpet music, string music and songs. During temple fairs, Peikuan is always the most eye-catching music troupe. As its organization is not as restricted as Nankuan, and even much flexible, it often heard in very many different music systems.

The Hakka music is divided into songs and instrument performance. The songs indicate folk songs, and the instrumental music Bayin. The folk songs narrating the clan's farming, tealeaf picking and other laborious works, and they are distinctive in the South and the North. Bayin has two forms, trumpet music and string music, both are popular in annual rituals, life ceremonies and temple fairs.

Taiwan is a place full of various traditional music. It is composed of the front stage, the performers, and the back stage, the musicians. The music used in the operas are Nankuan, Peikuan, Taiwan Opera songs and the Hakka music. Traditionally, the composition of an opera is to combine or verify the music available, and is not same as the way that Western operas are composed specifically by the composers. The combination of various music styles to complete an opera is called Chi Pa, such as Nakuan and Taiwan Opera; and the variation, according to the need to present the plot and characters, is called Ban Chiang, such as Peikuan.

Traditional music in Taiwan has long been a part of the people's daily life, and own tremendous amount of classics music. However, unfortunately, it was ignored by formal music education system, and even those who studied in music school would be unfamiliar with the traditional music. As the elder artists withered, the skills failed to hand down and outflow of audiences, the traditional Taiwanese music has faced a key turning point. To this very moment, efficient promotion has been most important than ever.

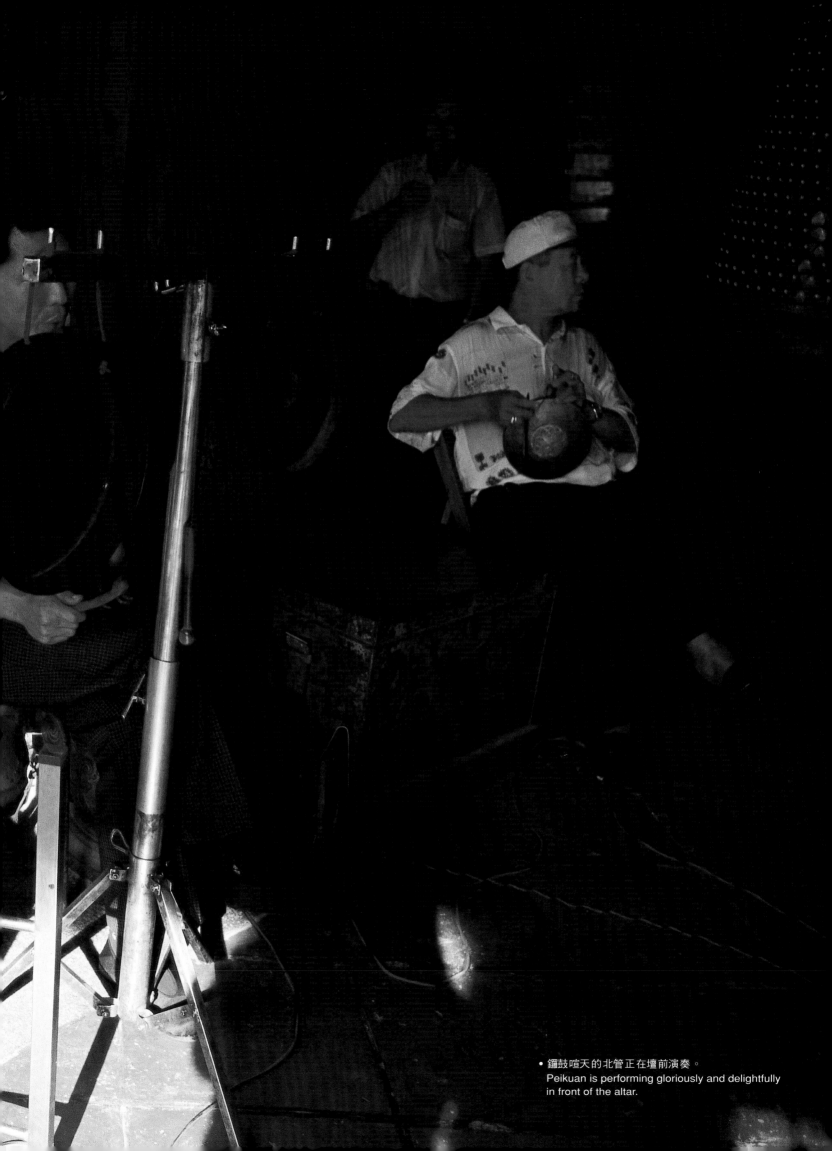

• 鑼鼓喧天的北管正在壇前演奏。
Peikuan is performing gloriously and delightfully in front of the altar.

南管

南管音樂是漢族音樂中古老的樂種，屬絲竹合奏之樂，展演型態有歌樂與器樂兩類。樂隊編制十分嚴謹，「上四管」由琵琶、三絃、洞簫、二絃、拍，五件樂器組合而成；「十音」則另加噯仔、響盞、四塊、叫鑼、雙音。演奏時各司其職，琵琶為樂團領奏，並負責彈奏骨幹音；洞簫在骨幹音的基礎加花穿梭，三絃襯托琵琶；二絃持續簫笙的綿延，拍則控制整體節奏。

NANKUAN

Nankuan is an age-old Han music, and is a mèlange of stringed and woodwind instruments. The presentation are categorized into song and instrument performances. Nankuan's team organization is very restricted, containing "shang si guan" (melodic instruments), such as pipa, three-string, vertical bamboo flute, two-string and clapper; and when it comes to "shi yin" (ten instruments), small trumpet, small gong, four bamboo blocks, single-sided gong, and brass bell are added. From those instruments, the exact organization of Nankuan is clearly presented: while performing, pipa plays the leading role and perform the major melody; the bamboo flute is used to decorates the major melody; the three-string flourish pipa music; two-string is an extension of flutes, and clappers helps to keep the rhythm.

- 太平歌的主要伴奏樂器有月琴、殼子絃、大廣絃、三絃（左一）、和絃、笛子等樂器。（圖1）
  Taipin Song (song of peace) is mainly accompanied by yue-chin, ke-zi string instrument, da-kuan string instrument, three-string instrument (on the left) and other string instruments. (photo 1)

- 南管噯仔的聲音纖細，不似北管嗩吶的粗曠。（圖2）
  Small trumpet has a intricate sound, and it is very different from Peikuan's suona horn. (photo 2)

- 十音合奏是南管的排場中，演奏人數最多的一種，中央一人手持拍，掌控樂隊的節拍。（圖3）
  "Shi yin" ensemble is the most grand performance in Nankuan music. The clapper performer, in the center, guides the rhythm of the troupe. (photo 3)

北管

北管音樂可說是台灣傳統音樂版圖最廣的樂種，漢族的傳統音樂除了南管之外，都與北管音樂有關。包括北管戲、歌仔戲、布袋戲、傀儡戲等劇種的後場，廟會慶典中的北管鼓吹陣，以及道教儀式的音樂等皆是。北管音樂貼近於人民的生活可見一般。

PEIKUAN

Peikuan covers the widest domain among the traditional music in Taiwan. Except Nankuan, all the Han traditional music is related to Peikuan, including that of the accompaniments of Peikuan Opera, Taiwan Opera, Taiwan Glove Puppets and String Puppet Show, as well as the Peikuan trumpet troupe in temple fairs and Taoist rituals. The closeness between Peikuan and the daily life of the people is clearly presented.

- 嗩吶，是北管鼓吹樂中形象最鮮明的樂器，也使用於道教儀式的後場（圖1），和廟會繞境的陣頭中（圖2,3）。
  Suona, the trumpet, is the most outstanding instruments in Peikuan trumpet music, and is used as the accompanying instrument in Taoist rituals (photo 1), temple fairs and divine inspecting occasions. (photos 2, 3)

- 北管戲後場的北管音樂，分為西皮和福路兩派，差別在於頭手使用的樂器。右一的樂師即為西皮派的頭手，手拉京胡（吊鬼仔），正為北管戲伴奏著。（圖4）
  The accompaniment of Peikuan Opera is categorized into "sipi" and "fulu"; the major difference is the instruments they use. The musician, the first on the right side, is the leader of sipi, who plays "inghu" to accompany for the Peikuan Opera. (photo 4)

• 哨角隊為迎神賽會開道，以震耳聲響掃除不潔。
The long brass trumpet troupe is leading the way for a
parade; it is said that the sound expel the evil force.

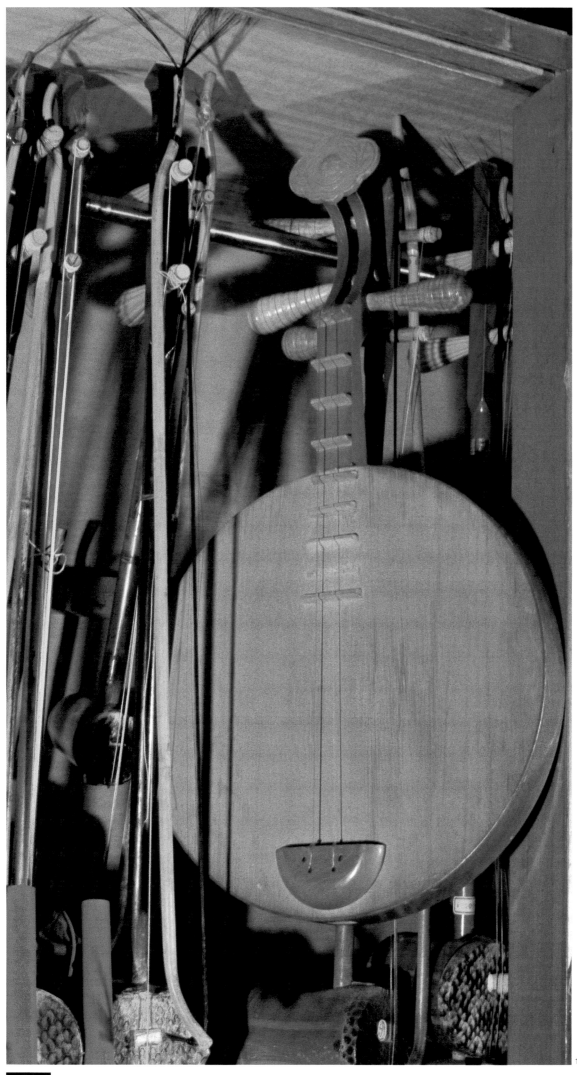

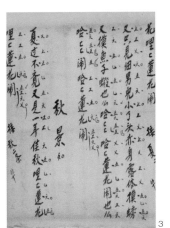

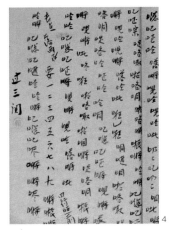

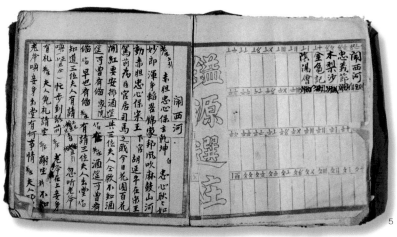

- 北管的樂器非常多樣，包括絃類樂器（圖1,2右）和吹類樂器的嗩吶（圖2左），常用櫃子來收納。圖2為瑞芳「得意堂」的樂器櫃。
  There are very many kinds of Peikuan instruments, including string instruments (photo 1 and 2 from right) and suona (photo 2 from left). They are well kept in cabinets, and photo 2 is the instrument cabinet of Te Yi Tan in Ruifang.

- 北管細曲抄本以工尺譜記寫旋律（圖3），但亦有僅記板撩的譜式。鑼鼓類抄本以狀聲字模擬音響（圖4）；戲曲總講僅記唱辭、說白、角色、上下場與過場樂器名。（圖5）
  Gongchepu is the major musical notation of Peikuan music (photo 3), however, there are notations only record the rhythm; the notations for gongs and drums are usually an imitation of sound (photo 4); for operas, the notations only take lyrics, narration, characters, on and off stage sequences and instruments played for the interval. (photo 5)

建築工藝

The Beauty
of Architecture

之美

建築工藝之美

審定◎林會承　國立台北藝術大學建築與古蹟研究所所長
撰文◎鄭昭民　中原大學建築研究所碩士

　　台灣位於大陸與海洋交會之處，為各種文化輻輳之地；在島嶼的時間長流上，共存著形式紛異的建築文化，是各個族群物質生活與精神生活之寄託。廣泛而言，台灣的傳統建築涵蓋了史前文化的考古遺址，以及陸續生活在島上的原住民、漢民族所建築的構造物，且兼容荷西、日本這些曾短暫停留的文化所引入的建築形式。由於台灣的住民多自中國大陸的閩、客移入，因此島上的傳統建築自然以漢式風格的數量居多，所呈現的工藝技術也較為豐富多樣。

　　一般漢式的傳統建築係由地盤、厝身、厝頂構成大致的輪廓。整體格局的擘畫、規制尺寸的掌握，須仰仗經驗豐富的大木司傅構思，並由其執行立柱搭梁的工作，以確立建築之骨架。此外，藉由土水司傅的協力，疊砌牆體、鋪設磚瓦，協力完成建築主體工程。

　　進一步裝修的工程，則由各類別的司傅分工負責，包含鑿花、打石、彩繪、堆花、剪黏、交趾乃至磚雕等等。透過司傅們的巧藝，運用不同的材料、技法表現，使得建築更添風采。鑿花即是應用在建築上的木雕工藝，常見於座斗、門窗、屏堵等木構件。同樣的，打石也採雕刻的技法裝飾，大多應用在需借重石材耐久、防潮特性的建築部位。上述二者均藉由線雕、膨堵、透雕、圓雕等種種的表現方式，讓原本單純的構材更形美觀。彩繪是在建築構件表面上色裝飾；彩繪之前先進行披麻布、補公灰的手續，並著手髹漆，使木構件外部形成保護層，再施以紋樣、圖案、書法，以增添人文氣息。

　　堆花、剪黏與交趾基本上均講究捏塑的技巧，以灰泥為材、木竹鐵絲為骨幹，做成平面壁堵或立體造像。而其相互間的差異在於，剪黏多了嵌貼的手續，需將所塑之粗坯黏上各色陶瓷片或玻璃片；而俗稱「尪仔」的交趾，則須經低溫釉燒的程序才能完成。此外，須經窯燒者還有磚雕一項，分為窯前雕、窯後雕兩種，前者於入窯前刻製，後者於磚上直接雕成，藉由拼組可做豐富的表現。

　　建築工藝的類型眾多，各工別的司傅們在長期經驗的傳承、累積之下，於相異的範疇裡各自建立準則。但無論是建築的擇址、坐向、佈局的取捨，乃至尺寸、顏色、裝飾的決定，仍遵循傳統空間觀念中禮制、風水、吉凶的規範，以追求安身立命上的慰藉。然而台灣畢竟是個多元文化的社會，在長時間的交流中，其他文化亦悄悄地滲入了漢文化，且被其吸收轉化。從建築工藝的技法、材料與主題種種細微之處，皆可見不同族群的風情。

麒麟回首是裙堵石雕常見的主題。
The Kylin is a frequent decorative stone carving in dados.

The Beauty of Architecture

Supervision: Lin Huei-cheng Director, Graduate School of Architecture and Historic Preservation, Taipei National University of the Arts

Text: Cheng Chao-min MA, Chung Yuan Christian University

Located on where the continent and the ocean meet, and where different cultures cross their paths, Taiwan, in the past long years, has coexisted diversified architecture forms, and spiritually and physically nourished all her people. Generally speaking, the great framing of traditional Taiwanese architecture widely includes prehistoric archaeological site, and constructions created by the Aborigine and the Han people who one after another lived on this land; and the styles, with the remnants left by those invaders and colonists, namely, the Dutch, the Spanish and the Japanese. However, since the predominating residents were from Fukien and Hakka from China, inescapably, the tradition of construction on this island is rather Han style than any other, and shows technical and artistic richness.

In general, a traditional Han style building is composed of the foundation, the body and the roof. As to the planning of integral layout and the controlling standards and measurements are contributed by most experienced carpenters, and also through his practice, key works, such as, posting pillars and fixing beams, are completed to assure structural precision. In addition, without the masons help, wall bricklaying and roof tiling can never be achieved.

Further fixing-ups are managed by different craftsmen according to the nature of the works, ranging from wood carving, stone carving, color painting, mortar shaping, ceramics cutting and pasting decoration, koji pottery, brick carving and etc. With all those artists' excellent skills, materials, expression, the architectures are more brilliant than ever.

Woodcarving is mostly applied in embellishing plinths, doors and windows, screen walls and other wooden components. Similarly, stone carving is an important part of traditional Taiwanese architecture for duration and moisture-proof. The above-mentioned carving skills are to enhance the texture and appearance, and are categorized into line carving, relief-like semi-three-dimensional carving, openwork,

three-dimensional carving and so forth.

Color painting is to add colors and patterns to the components. The first step of painting is to check the linen firmly stretched on the surface and the layers of mortar on the surface of the linen, and then evenly lacquer it to form a protection and smooth surface layer for painting. The patterns include lines, calligraphy and other decorations that would increase artistic flavor.

The major skills of mortar shaping, ceramics cutting and pasting and koji pottery are related to exquisite kneading and molding. Wood, bamboo and iron wire are used as supporting skeleton, and mortar as the body, and are made into flat wall decorations and three-dimensional images. However, there are crucial differences in their making. Ceramic cutting and pasting focus on cutting ready-made ceramics of all colors into pieces and assemble them into desired patterns; koji pottery art, such as low-temperature kilning. Last but not the least, also related to kilning, brick carving can be carving before kilning and carving after kilning; both are pieced together into richly artistic expression.

Architecture techniques are diverse and numerous. Craftsmen of each field are nourished by precedents and their own learning and practice, and therefore develop respective standards. However, there are still common and traditional confinements of courtesy, fengshui (geomancy), the norm of good and bad luck, directions and overall arrangement of space, as well as size, colors, decorations to be as their essential guidelines to follow, so to achieve a sense of spiritual stability and physical comfort. As the fact that Taiwan's distinctive cultural diversification, after century long communicating, other cultures quietly permeated into Han culture, and eventually absorbed and converted; examples of those foreign and subtle details are seen in the techniques, the using of materials and the subject matter.

● 傳統建築 是民間藝術的殿堂。
The traditional architecture is one of
the showcases of the folk art.

大木

在傳統漢式木構造建築中，大木為整體之骨幹。透過大木司傅的經驗與巧思，決定建築的佈局、規模，確立構材的形式、尺寸；並且依靠精準的施工技術，將柱、梁、通、楹等主要結構，與補強、聯繫的組件，以榫卯的方式搭接，完成建築的骨幹。

MAJOR SUPPORT

The traditional wooden structure of Han style architecture, major wooden support is the backbone of the body. By means of the experiences and skills of the carpenter specializing in wooden support, the layout and scale are decided, and the form and size are firmed. According to their precise construction techniques, pillars, beams, horizontal short beams, and the beams connected directly to the ceiling are connected and enhanced to form the strong frame of the architecture, by using tenon techniques.

• 傳統建築在各類空間採用的木構架形式皆不相同：拜亭常採四架楹的捲朋頂（右圖）；正殿常見三通五瓜的架棟（圖1）；戲臺則以斗栱挑疊做成結網（圖2）；步口的員光、斗座雕飾華麗（圖3）。
Traditional architectures show different wooden structural frames, in accordance with their functions; for example, the roof, in a shape like a cut-half tube, without the ridge and supported by four pillars is usually seen in the Worshiping Hall (photo, right); the Main Hall shows three beams and five pumpkin shape support (photo 1); the Stage's wood brackets stake into cobweb pattern ceiling (photo 2); the long carved board of the cornice and the indirect beam supports show splendid carving. (photo 3)

● 鹿港龍山寺戲臺繁複華麗的八角形結網。
The resplendent octagon cobweb pattern ceiling of the stage in Long Shan Temple, Lukang.

- 連續出挑的斗栱與成列的吊筒，儼然自成韻律。
（圖1）
Continuous wood brackets and the array of hanging
pillar look rhythmic. (photo 1)

- 修長的趖瓜筒與肥短的金瓜筒相映成趣。（圖2,3）
Slender and portly and short pumpkin pillar make an
interesting contrast. (photos 2, 3)

- 斗栱為漢式傳統建築中相當特殊的構造系統，以簡單
的升、斗承載栱及翹，組合出多端的變化。圖為裝飾
性濃厚的如意斗栱。（圖4,5）
Wood brackets are very special structure in Han style
architecture, and by using different kinds of bow-
shaped support, form a diverse structure. Photo 4
and 5 are decorative good luck ru yi wood brackets.

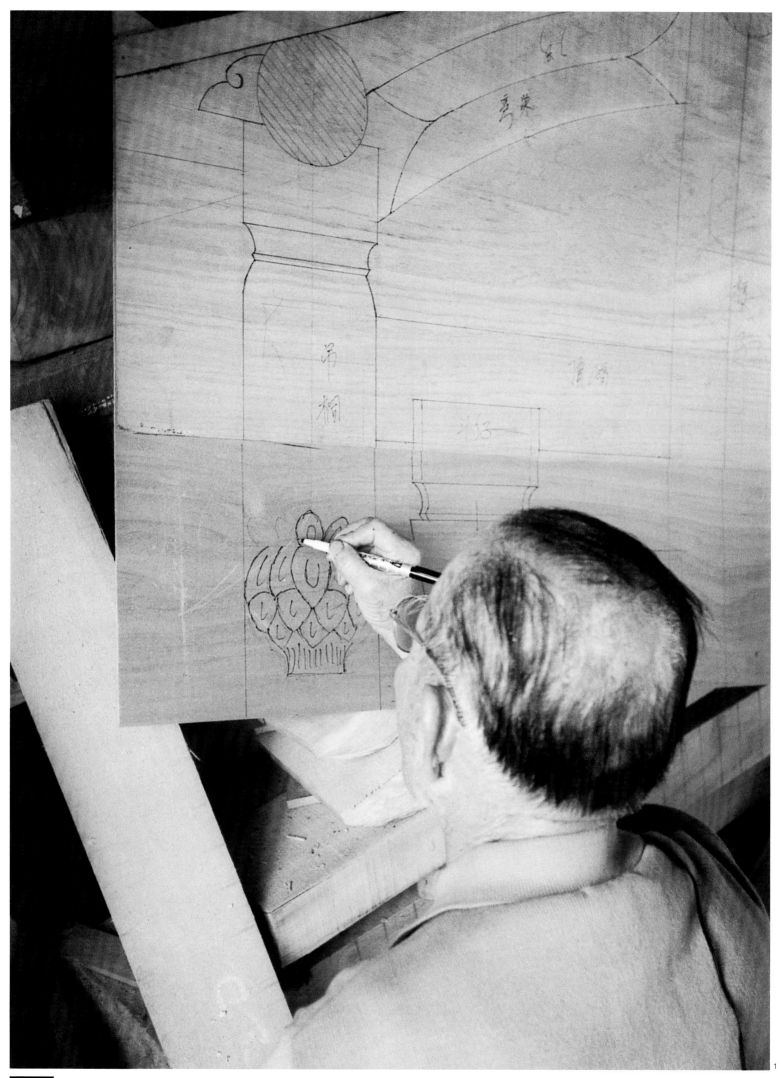

● 早期大木司傅以篙尺、卦書做為施工的準則；晚期則因日本人的影響，先繪建築圖面（圖1），再依圖面進行構件的施工（圖2-5）。

Beam carpenters in early years used Kao Che, a flat ruler with different standard scales for each material and the Eight Diagrams in Chinese mythology as the standard of the construction. Later, due to the Japanese influence, they adapted to draw the design first (photo 1) and follow the design when built the components. (photos 2-5)

鑿花

鑿花，是應用在建築上的木雕工藝，將具功能性的構材加以雕鑿修飾。原則上，直接承重的，如柱、梁、通、楹，僅施以線腳；間接承重的，如斗座，是以浮雕為主；而輔助、聯繫的構材或屏罩、門窗等，則不受限制。藉由種種形式、主題互異的裝飾，軟化了建築原本單調的框架。

WOOD CARVING

Wood carving is a skill used to beautify the functional components. Basically, line patterns are put on those components carrying weights directly, such as pillar, beam; and reliefs are applied in those components indirect carry the weights, such as indirect beam supports. As to those support or connecting units, doors and windows are not confined by the principles. By using decorations from various different forms and themes, the monotonous frames are softened.

- 插角，或稱托木、雀替，是承托梁柱接合處的構件。其造形多樣，以鰲魚（圖1,2）、翔鳳、仙人（圖3）最為常見。

  Cha jiao is a device for supporting the connection of a beam and pillar. It has various forms, such as frequent appeared creature with dragon's head and fish's body (photos 1, 2), flying phoenix, immortals. (photo 3)

- 斗座，為上承斗栱，下接大通、梁之構件。有走獸造形，如龍（圖4）、虎、獅；也有水族造型，如蝦、蟹（圖5）；以及人物、花草等。

  The indirect beam supports carry the weight of wood brackets from above, and connect to the components of beams. Some are shaped as animals, such as dragons (photo 4), tigers, lions, and some are modeled as aquatic creatures, such as prawns and crabs (photo 5), as well as people and floras.

彩繪

彩繪，如字面所見，涵蓋「彩」與「繪」兩部分。「彩」即上色，由基層的處理至表面油漆皆屬之；「繪」指繪畫，包含圖案的設計、圖面的描繪與書法。在建築中主要施作於梁通及壁面，兼具裝飾美化、保護構材的功能，並且寓有驅邪、祈福、教化及闡明心志之意涵。

COLOR PAINTING

Color painting, as the name literally indicates, contains colors and painting. Color is to add colors to it, from primary process to surface paint; paining means drawing, including pattern designing, painting and calligraphy. In a building, it is mainly applied in beams and walls, both for decorating and protecting the components, as well as driving away the evil force, praying for blessing, educating and inspiring people.

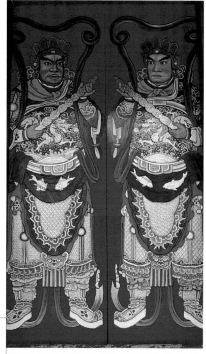
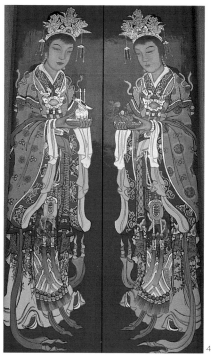

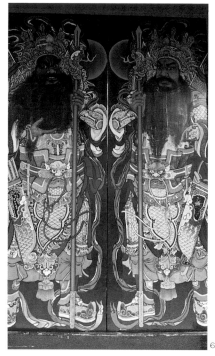

- 門神彩繪的主題取決於廟宇的主祀神，佛祖、觀音多採韋馱、伽藍（圖1,3,5）或四大天王（圖2,7）；媽祖則可見宮娥（圖4）、太監；其他則以神荼、鬱壘（圖6）或秦叔寶、尉遲恭最為普遍。

The theme of door-god painting is depending on the major god the temple contributed to. For Buddha and Guanyin, Wei Tuo and Jia Lan (photos 1, 3, 5) or the Four Great Generals are painted (photos 2, 7); for Matze, there are young maids (photo 4), eunuchs, as to the other door-gods, Shen Tu, Yu Lei (photo 6) or Chin Shu Bao and Yu Chi Gong are most frequently seen.

- 台南畫師蔡草如與其作品的合影，背景門神為《封神榜》內職司「風調雨順」之四大天王中的魔禮青、魔禮海。（圖7）

Artist Tsai Chao Ru, from Tainan, and his works. The door-gods in the background are, based on the story of "Feng Shen Bang" (Rewarding the Gods), Mo Li Ching and Mo Li Hai, the gods granting favorable weather, and two of the gods of the Four Great Generals. (photo 7)

• 潘麗水所繪「鍾馗迎妹回娘家」。
"Chong Kui Welcoming Younger Sister Home"
by Pan Li Shui.

1

2

- 台南開基靈佑宮廟內三十六官將壁畫局部。呈現神祇纖柔、剛烈互異的性格特質。（圖1）
  Details of Thirty-six General Gods fresco in Kai Ji Ling You Temple, Tainan. The gods' gentle and unyielding natures giving very strong contrasts. (photo 1)

- 「武侯奉表」壁堵畫作。描繪三國時代諸葛亮夜呈出師表的情節，透過表彰「忠」之傳統情操，達到教化的目的。（圖2）
  The dado paining "Wu Hou Feng Biao", depicting Zhu Ge Liang, Three King-dom period, presented his plea of dispatching troops to fight one night. This is to honor the nobility of Loyalty and to inspire people. (photo 2)

- 台南府城人文薈萃，著名畫師各擅勝場。圖為蔡草如的「雉雞聽法轉人世」（圖3）、潘麗水的「八仙大鬧東海」（圖4）及陳玉峰的「舜耕歷山」（圖5）。
  Tainan is a very culturally developed city, and there are very many famous painters. Photo 3 shows Tasi Chao Ru and his "Pheasant listens to Buddha dharma and turns to human"; photo 4 is "Eight Immortals rumble the East Sea" by Pan Li Shui and "'Shun Plows in Li Mountain" by Chen Yu Feng.

磚雕

磚雕是於紅磚上施以雕飾的工藝，一般分為窯前雕、窯後雕兩種。窯前雕是在坯土入窯前先刻上紋樣，再行燒製，因形體、色澤不易掌握，故難度頗高。窯後雕則是直接取紅磚進行雕刻，表現形式以淺雕為多。於建築的壁堵、牆基收邊，或轉角處，偶可見磚雕的作品。

BRICK CARVING

Brick carving is an art form applied on red bricks. There are carving before kilning and carving after kilning; the former is to carve on the molded clay with patterns before put into a kiln, and this is more difficult than the other as it is hard to control its shape and colors; and the latter is to carve directly on ready-made bricks, mostly are relief patterns. They are seen on the dado, wall base or some corners of traditional buildings.

• 斑駁的磚雕蘊含著滄桑之感，然而透過幾何形式的排列、組砌，卻又展現出迥然不同的意趣。（圖1-6）
The pied brick carving implies subtle and ancient atmosphere, but when arranged geometrically, they show very different zest. (photos 1-6)

2

3

4

5

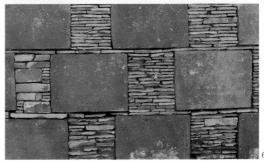

6

石雕

雕刻所用的石材，須以質地細緻而硬度適中者為佳；然台灣早期的石材供需仰賴唐山的輸入，以青斗石、白石、礱石為主。而後本島所產的石材，則以觀音山石為大宗。一般而言，石雕的施作須經多人分工，先由頭手負責構思形體、佈局，並雕鑿粗坯，再由二手接續，進行修飾完工。

STONE CARVING

The best stones for carving are those with mild hardness. In the old time, Taiwan relied on stones imported from China, mainly Green stone, white stone and grain stone. Later, it was changed to local products, and stones from Guanyin Mountain were the most popular. Generally speaking, each stone carving is processed by several people. It starts with layout designing and primary chiseling, all by master craftsman, and finishes the rest by his assistant with detail works.

- 石質柱珠原為防止木柱受潮腐朽而設，而在長時間的演變下，發展出眾多形式，如蓮座形、圓形、四角形、六角形、八角形等。（圖1-6）
  The stone plinth was invented to prevent the wooden pillars to be damaged by dampness, and through long period of time, eventually developed into different forms, such as lotus, round, square, hexagonal and octagonal plinth. (photos 1-6)

- 石雕龍柱的龍身係貼附著圓形或八角形柱盤旋而下，間以雲紋點綴，整體顯得渾圓而流暢；而昂揚的龍首與賁張的龍爪，更增添了幾分力道。（圖7,8）
  The dragon of a stone carving "dragon pillar" spirals downward from the top of a round or octagonal pillar, and is decorated with cloud patterns. It is perfectly round and smooth as a whole, and the strength is enhanced by the upward dragon head and stretching dragon claws. (photos 7, 8)

1

2

3

4

5

6

7

8

• 大門門框前的門枕石上方，常常安置有石鼓或石獅；因所在位置醒目，石鼓或石獅的造型、雕工皆相當講究。（圖1-5）

Above the stone pillow in the gate frame, stone drums or stone lions are often seen; and due to the eye-catching position, the drums or lions, with excellent design and intricate carving, are very exquisite. (photos 1-5)

• 在石雕的技法中，有圓雕、透雕、平雕、膨堵與
線雕之別；一般的壁堵多採膨堵（圖1,2,4）或平
雕（圖3）的表現方式，其間偶而摻以透雕。

There are three-dimensional carving, openwork,
flat carving (also three-dimensional, but the surface appear to be flat), relief-like semi-three-
dimensional carving and line carving. Relief-like
semi-three-dimensional carving (photos 1, 2, 4) or
flat carving (photo 3) are the most used skill for
decorating dadoes, and some are mixed with
openwork.

- 透雕的石窗，訴說的是「三國演義」內的征戰情節，運用分段敘述的構圖方式，表現出豐富的層次與緊湊的場面。（圖1）
  This openwork stone window tells the story of wars in The Three Kingdoms period, by using sectional pictorial narration, and rich arrangements and well-knitted scenes are perfectly expressed. (photo 1)

- 取材自歷史演義、神話傳說或文學典故的人物，透過石雕的呈現，其表情與身形十分傳神，毛髮與衣摺等細部亦纖毫畢現。（圖2-4）
  The protagonists from famous historical romance, mythic legend and classic literature are relived through stone carving and the expressions and shapes vivid, and even hair and plaits are lifelike. (photos 2-4)

剪黏

剪黏，或稱剪花，是利用木竹、鐵絲紮製骨架，灰泥捏塑成形，再以上有釉色的陶瓷碎片黏貼於表面；是一項結合了堆花、彩繪、鑲嵌等傳統技術的工藝。隨著材料的革新、技術的簡化，表面也陸續改採彩色玻璃或淋搪片現代材質。目前，在廟宇的屋頂所見堂皇亮麗的裝飾，多運用剪黏手法製作。

CERAMICS CUTTING AND PASTING

Ceramics cutting and pasting is sometimes called cutting flowers. Wood, bamboo and iron wire are used as supporting skeleton, and mortar as the body. Colorful ceramic shards are pasted on the clay. It is, indeed, an art combined with ceramic shaping, color painting and inlaying. Follow the renovation of materials and the simplification of technology, ceramic shards are eventually replaced by stained glass. Nowadays, those gorgeous decorations on the temple rooftops are most done with the skill of ceramics cutting and pasting.

- 脊堵以剪黏技法做成人物帶騎之齣頭為裝飾，脊頂為麒麟馱八卦及雙龍。（圖1）
  What on the roof frieze are colorful riding animal figurines made by ceramics cutting and pasting techniques; the figures on the roof ridge are kylin (Chinese unicorn) carrying the Eight Diagrams and double dragon. (photo 1)

- 脊頂中央若安置寶塔、寶珠，則為「雙龍拜塔」或「雙龍搶珠」。（圖2-4）
  When a roof ridge is placed with a pagoda and a ball, it is called "double dragons worshipping the pagoda" or "double dragons fighting for the ball." (photos 2-4)

• 台北保安宮的牌頭人物及串角祥鳳之剪黏。
The ceramics cutting and pasting figure and phoenix work on the end of the hang ridge in Pao-an Temple, Taipei.

4

• 牌頭的剪黏常以人物故事做為題材。點綴有樹木、岩石的戶外
征戰場面為武齣（圖1）；人物背後有亭台、樓閣者，則多屬
文齣。（圖2,3）
The ceramics cutting and pasting legendary figures are frequently used to decorate the hanging roof ends; with trees and
rock are mostly warfare scene (photo 1), and with pavilions and
towers are mostly romantic stories (photos 2, 3).

• 屋頂規帶末端稱為串角。做抽象的草仔尾隨勢揚起、捲曲，顯
得輕盈而流暢；搭配昇龍，更增躍動之感。（圖4）
The end of the hanging roof ridge is called "chuan jiao",
shaped in abstract raising and curling of grass leaves. When
collocate with spiraling dragons, the leaping rhythm is ever
high-spirited. (photo 4)

堆花

堆花，是使用灰泥塑形，表層再上色修飾之工藝。由於材質容易表現、施作簡便，堆花廣泛地被運用在建築裝飾上，例如：壁堵、水車堵、檐口落水、山牆以及屋頂上，皆可見其蹤跡。因所在部位的不同，又有半立體或立體等多樣的表現方式。

MORTAR SHAPING

Mortar Shaping uses clay as its body, and paint on the surface for embellishment. Due to the material is easy to mold, and the practice is simple, ceramics shaping is widely applied as architectural decorations, such as on dadoes, gables and rooftops. They can be either semi-three dimensional or fully three dimensional in form, depending on the location they are put on.

- 在漢民族的空間觀念中，白虎象徵右方、西方。因此在廟宇步口的右側壁堵，常有以老虎、伏虎羅漢或定光古佛降虎為題材的堆花，藉此隱喻其方位。（圖1）
  According to Han's concept of space, white tiger symbolizes right side and the west, so that on the right side dado of a temple's eave, there is always Mortar Shaping work of a tiger, and Lo Han yielding a tiger, or a tiger surrendering to Din Kuang Buddha, to indicate the direction. (photo 1)

- 半立體堆花的運用，可見於山牆頂端的懸魚惹草及磬牌（圖2-4）；而立體的堆花，如仙姑乘鶴巧妙地呈現屋脊末端起翹之勢（圖5）。
  Semi-three dimensional Mortar Shaping is easily seen on the top of a gable as crest decoration and mostly are pattern of curly grasses and chime stone (photos 2-4); three-dimensional Mortar Shaping are well-demonstrated by the "female immortal riding a crane" figure that ingeniously reinforces the upwardly raised roof end (photo 5).

交趾陶

交趾陶源自中國的閩、粵地區，為低溫燒製的彩釉軟陶，其製作程序須經練土、捏塑、乾胚、挖空、整修、素燒、及多次的釉燒，技巧繁複而難度甚高。在台灣傳統的漢式建築中，常做為壁堵、水車堵、墀頭及屋頂的裝飾；而最負盛名的司傳，為清代嘉義的葉王。

KOJI POTTERY

Koji was originally from Fukien and Canton provinces. It is colorfully glazed soft pottery, kilned under lower temperature. The procedures, by sequence, are kneading, molding, drying, hollowing, modifying, first kiln without glaze, plus several times of kiln with glaze. The procedure is complicated and difficult. It is often used in dadoes and rooftop. The most famous craftsman was Yeh Wan, during Chia Ching reign, Ching Dynasty.

• 以半立體之交趾陶裝飾的壁堵，取材自抽象的螭虎、卷草圖案，或具象的動物、植物、器物等，以求吉祥平安之意涵。
（圖1-4）
Dado decorated by semi-three dimensional koji. The patterns include abstract dragon-tiger, curly grasses, or concrete animals, plants, utensils, all for signs of peace and tranquility. (photos 1-4)

1

● 佳里震興宮的葉王作品「憨番抬厝角」。（圖1,2）
"The Fool Trying to Raise the House" by Yeh Wan,
Chen Shing Temple, Chia Li. (photos 1, 2)

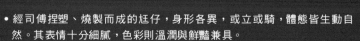

• 經司傅捏塑、燒製而成的尪仔，身形各異，或立或騎，體態皆生動自然。其表情十分細膩，色彩則溫潤與鮮豔兼具。
The figurines made by experienced craftsmen are very vivid. They are different in shapes. Standing or riding, they all look lively with delicate facial expression and lifelike colors.

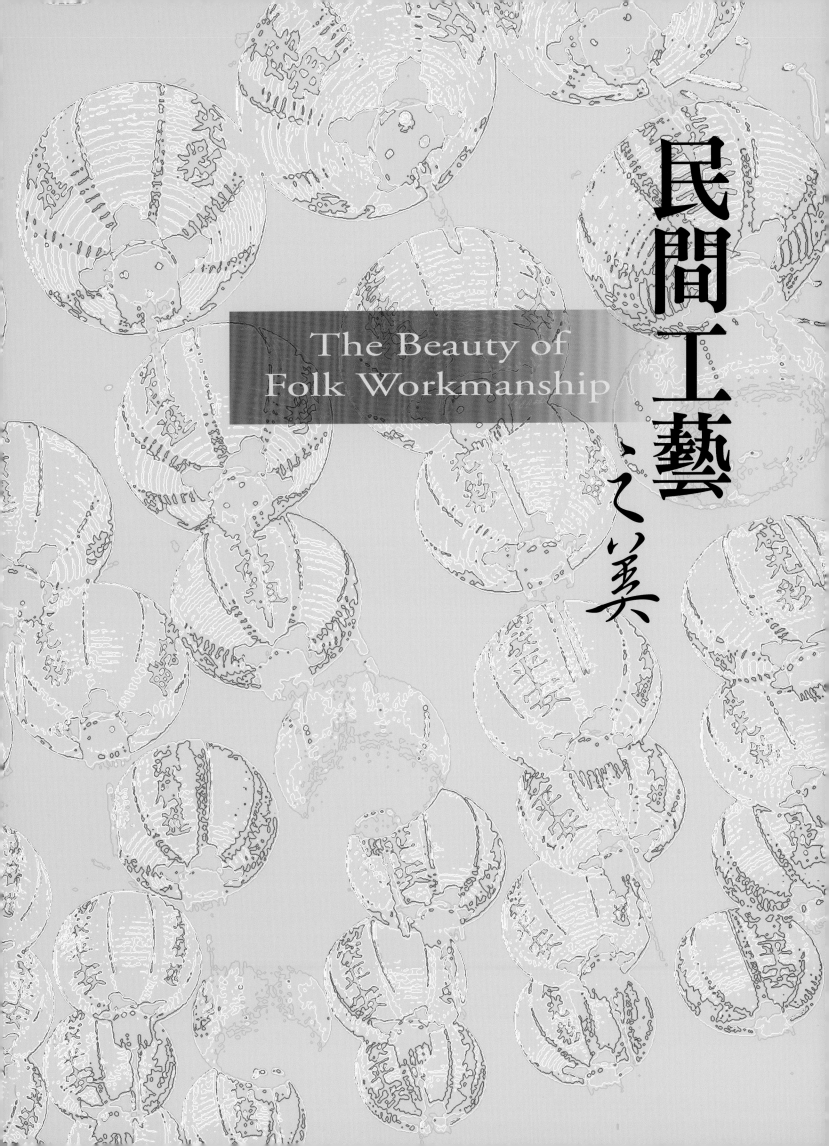

民間工藝

之美

The Beauty of
Folk Workmanship

民間工藝之美

審定◎江韶瑩　國立台北藝術大學傳統藝術研究所所長
撰文◎陳怡方　國立台北藝術大學傳統藝術研究所碩士

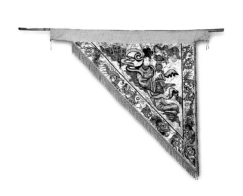

融匯了使用的功能、材質的美感和技藝的巧妙，是「工藝」的特質與價值所在。而「民間工藝」，一方面保存了傳統的生活文化，另一方面則立足於常民生活的真實體驗與真誠感情，而與宮廷、貴族的工藝有所區隔。

民間工藝的起源和發展都與民眾日常生活緊密連繫。工藝製作者不僅是完成符合實用目的的工藝品，還會在製作過程中加入巧思，呈現豐富的視覺效果。因而，工藝品不只滿足生活的便利與舒適，更在使用時增添生活中愉悅的感受。民間工藝可能因為社會與交易供銷需求，發展成地域性的工藝產業。這樣的工藝，普遍能結合地方得天獨厚的自然與人文條件，並使用質地美好且適用的工藝材料，深具地區特色。

台灣的民間工藝，就涵蓋了「生活需求」與「地域特色」兩者，從而發展出眾多的類別。一方面是生活日用所需的工藝製作，展現在食、衣、住、行、信仰、娛樂等層面：食的方面，如竹編的蒸籠、榭籃，木製的飯桶、糕粿餅模，陶瓷製的碗盤，鐵鑄打的菜刀、鐵壺。衣的方面，如印染的衫裙、包袱巾，刺繡的八仙綵、繡旗。住的方面，如木製或竹籐製的家具，或香爐、燭臺，還有地毯、草編的蓆墊。行的方面，如轎子，舟筏，穿著的木屐、繡鞋，供照明用的燈籠、觀賞花燈。此外，還有普遍應用於民間信仰等精神生活層面的工藝製作，如神像、製香、祭具；以及與歲時或生命禮儀相關的工藝，如糊紙、版印；還有娛樂表演用的各式樂器、銅鑼、戲偶製作等。

另一方面，地方特色產業，種類繁多，例如陶瓷器在鶯歌、南投、六甲；木家具在大溪、豐原、鹿港；竹藤製品在竹山、關廟；草編在通霄、苑裡、大甲、學甲；神佛具在鹿港、嘉義、北港等，不勝枚舉。原住民工藝則以泰雅、賽夏族的織布；布農、鄒族的皮革工藝；魯凱、排灣族的刺繡、陶壺、琉璃珠以及達悟族的漁舟、土偶等，均深受歡迎。

因應生活需求，民間工藝會隨著時代的發展而演變，有些工藝被新的工業產品所取代、汰換；也有因應新的生活環境而產生的新類型工藝。儘管如此，始終不變的是工藝製作者在工作中的專注與敬業。民間工藝匠師往往都有含蓄而內斂的真情，透過雙手注入工藝品；長年浸潤其中，不為功名利祿、不斷精進的手藝，造就了工藝品的動人形貌。他們製作出的工藝品不僅細緻、更是恰如其份。工藝作家的心情、動作與工藝品渾然成為一體；在純熟、洗鍊的構造與質感中，透露出的是一種全然的圓滿。

木桶曾是家家必備的生活用品。
The wood buckets were of daily supplies.

The Beauty of Folk Workmanship

Supervision: Chiang Shao-ying — Director, Graduate School of Folk Culture & Arts, Taipei National University of the Arts

Text: Chen Yi-fang — MA, Graduate School of Folk Culture & Arts, Taipei National University of the Arts

The nature and value of workmanship is a mélange of how ingeniously the material, techniques and the functions are combined. The folk workmanship preserves the traditional livelihood cultures, on a base of true experiences of, and genuine affection to, daily life of the common people, and is distinct from that of the court and the nobility.

The origin and development of folk workmanship intimately attach to daily life. The artisans produce not just practical utensils for livelihood needs, but inject their artistry and ingenuity in their productions to reinforce visual delight. Therefore, the handicrafts make life more colorful and rich, while the need of conveniences and comforts are satisfied. The handicrafts might well develop into regional specialties as the customs of the communities and supply and marketing of the area. Such a feature is usually integrated with the locally exceptional natural resources and human ecology, and proper and quality materials are made use; thus, the local flavor is within.

Combing the livelihood demand and regionalism, the folk handicrafts of Taiwan have a large classification and are roughly but suitably categorized into two groups.

The first, the productions for daily life, include utensils for the cookery, such as weaved bamboo steamer, weaved basket with cover, wooden cooked rice buckets, rice cake molds, ceramic bowls and plates, as well as cast iron choppers and pot; clothing and ritual cloth products, such as printed and dyed blouses and skirts, cloth wrappers, embroidered Eight Immortals banners and pennants; commodities for daily life, such as wooden or rattan furniture, incense burners, candleholders, carpets, straws mats and so on; instruments for mobility, such as palanquins, boats, rafts, clogs, even lanterns for the purposes of illumination, enjoyment and rituals. What is more, there are handicrafts especially made for folk beliefs and spiritual life, for example, deity statues, incense, worshipping utensils, and productions for festivals and ceremonies, such as paper-pasting and block printing, and varied music instruments manufacturing, gong making, puppet producing and others, for recreational purposes.

And the second is emphasized by local industries that developed mostly from its natural resources, to give some examples, ceramics in Yinge, Nantou and Liujia; wooden furniture in Dasi, Fengyuan and Lugang; rattan products in Chushan and Kuanmiao; straws weaving in Tongsiao, Yuanli, Dachia and Shuechia; implements for divine worshipping in Lugang, Chiayi and Peigan. There are rich productions from the Aboriginal peoples of Taiwan, such as Atayal and Saisyat's textiles, Bunun and Tsou's leather products, Ruaki and Paiwan's embroideries, pottery pots and lazurite beads, and Tao's fishing canoes and earth figurines.

Answering to the livelihood needs, the folk workmanship advances with the trails of the changes and development of the day, and some have been eventually replaced by new products, and some have evolved into new models. Nevertheless, what remains unchanged is the single-mindedness and the respect and ethics to their professions. The cordial feeling and introspection of the folk handicraftsmen are embedded in their articles through their work. Their patience and being aloof from fames and riches, as wee as the will of self-improvements, have made their artworks ever intriguing. Their works are intricate and proper. The moods, techniques and works of the handicraftsmen are combined as one, and in the skillful and mature structures and textures, the perfection is consummated.

● 面容慈祥的媽祖神像。
Kind and merciful Ma Tzu.

神像

神像雕造工藝，與宗教信仰緊密結合。「刻佛司傅」或「妝佛司傅」是民間對於神像雕造、粧身者的稱呼，意指為神明裝飾面容的匠師。司傅依神明的事蹟、法器與神格，雕造各具姿態的造型、坐姿、神態，以呈現神像的性格和顏貌。司傅的細緻巧思與精湛雕工，充分展現人間神明的神聖莊嚴。

DIVINE STATUE

The divine statues skills are closely related to religions. The sculptors of divine statues are respectfully addressed as the master of divine sculpturing and the master of divine sprucing, to indicate their professional skills for decorating the divine appearances. The masters, according to the deeds, the instruments the deities use and their divine ranks, sculpt the deities in various postures with different facial expressions, in order to present the deities' personalities and looks properly. Through the exquisite skills and ingenuities, the solemnity of both the artists and the deities are well interpreted.

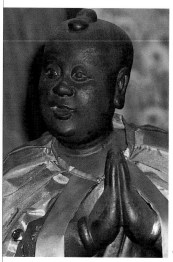

• 神像的造型繁多，各具特色，有面容純真的金童（圖1）；有與傳說故事緊密相扣的媽祖駕前護衛：千里眼（圖2）、順風耳（圖6）；有面部神情莊嚴、內斂端正、慈悲圓融、威風八面、氣勢懾人者，如四海龍王（圖3）、陳永華（圖4）、媽祖（圖7）；還有氣勢磅礡、龍首造型的東海龍王（圖5）。

The appearances of the divine statues are tremendously diverse. There is the Gold Child (photo 1) with innocent look, legendary loyal guards of Ma Tzu, Chian Li Yan (a farsighted god, photo 2) and Shun Feng Er (a god who hears voices a long way off, photo 6). What is more, some solemn, some demure, some gentle, some awe-inspiring, some forceful, and examples are the Dragon King of the Sea (photo 3), Chen Yuan Hua (photo 4), Ma Tzu (photo 7); and the powerful East Sea Gragon King, with human body and dragon head (pohto 5).

- 神像製作的過程，從清淨儀式開始，經過擇日、開斧、雕成大樣（粗胚）、
定型、修光、入神儀式、修整細部、磨光、上色、安金（上漆線）、開面、
開光點眼、安座供奉乃至完成。（圖1-4）

The process of divine statue making starts from purification, and followed
by fixing the date, initialing the use of ax, primary carving, modeling,
trimming, asking god to reside, polishing, painting, emphasizing the lines,
varnishing the face, painting the pupils (opening the eyes), and finally, fixing in the specific place for worshipping. (photos 1-4)

- 神像背部預留的圓洞是為「入神」而設。入神時，依據神明性格、神像大
小的不同及主家的要求，將香火、虎頭蜂、七寶、五穀、五色線等靈物填
入洞中，再用香薰之，並封閉洞孔，然後上漆、安金。一般人相信，如此
一來神像就具有超自然的靈力。（圖3）

There is a hole in the back of each statue and it is for the ritual of asking
god to reside into the statue. During the ritual, according to the personality of the god, and the size of the statue, as well as the requirements of the
worshipper (the owner of the statue), the host will insert a small spell bag,
a wasp, seven treasures (pearl, agate, amber, gold, silver...), five grains and
five strings of different colors into the hole. After waving incense smoke to
it, and the hold is sealed and painted, as well as drawing the lines. It is
believed that the statues, after such a process, have the supernatural
power. (photo 3)

製香

不論是線香或是盤香，皆香煙裊裊，在眾生焚香祝禱之際，可以上達天庭，為神明聞問。民間最常用的線香，以竹篾為骨幹，香料附著在竹枝之上。香料的調配相當講究，多以檀香、沈香、楠木磨成香粉末，再配上中藥材，才能在燃香時散發溫和而持久的香味。

JOSS STICK

No matter from incense sticks or incense coils, the wavering smoke serves as a medium that carries the worshipper's prayer to the gods in the Heaven. The most used is incense sticks, with very slender bamboo strips as the stems that the incense powder is adhered to. The mix of incense powder is very fastidious, and the most frequently used elements are powders prepared from sandalwood, agalloch and nato, plus various Chinese herbs; and the make like this will assure the durable fragrance while burning.

- 「做香末（肉）」是使線香附著香料的製作程序。過程中以雙手的力量，靈活地將一把一把竹枝用水沾濕、攤灑張開成扇形，然後沾裹黏劑，並重複、均勻的沾黏香料於香腳上。（圖 1-3）

  Making the flesh for incense is a procedure to adhere fragrant powders to the sticks. One will see, in the process, how the handicraftsmen use both of their hands, and swiftly wet the bundles of sticks, and spread them out in fan shape to apply special paste to the stick. Then, the powders are evenly and repeated adhere to the sticks. (photos 1-3)

- 「曬香腳」是製作線香最後的一個階段。香腳通常染成吉利的紅色，染好後將一捆捆香倒過來放置，以待曬乾，即可包裝出售。（圖 4）

  Drying up the feet of the sticks is the last step of incense stick manufacturing. Here, the handles, where, for holding, no powder is attached to, are dyed red. And bundles of already-made incense sticks are put in shallow and round sieve to dry up totally. After packing up, they are ready for sell. (photo 4)

刺繡

刺繡工藝品色彩繽紛，圖案精緻，散發喜氣吉祥的熱鬧氣息。刺繡品分為宗教性與日常生活使用兩種。前者如涼傘、神衣、轎布、頭旗、神案之桌裙、道士服等。後者如喜慶用的門頭彩、八仙彩，家裡懸掛的畫聯、繡屏與門簾，以及昔日穿帶的霞披、劍帶、手帕、荷包、肚兜、摺裙、童帽及繡花鞋等，種類繁多。

EMBROIDERY

Embroideries, with the delightful color and exquisite patterns, often distribute joyous, auspicious, vigorous and bustling air. They are almost a must for both religious and daily use; the former includes canopies, clothing for gods, cover cloth for palanquins, leading banners, the skirts of worshipping desks and the Taoists' ritual garbs; and the latter includes exterior above-door banners for joyous events, the Eight Immortals banners, embroidered paintings, screens and door drapery for interior use, as well as ancient wedding dress, sword belts, handkerchiefs, purses, undergarments, plait skirts, hats for children, and embroidered shoes and very many other items.

- 長條形的頭旗常作為陣頭的前導，代表某寺廟或神明子弟社團、館閣的標幟。旗面上常以金蔥、銀蔥線，繡以立體的雙龍拜塔狀紋樣，簇擁著中央的名稱。（圖1,2）
  Long trips of banners are used in the leading team of a parade. They are embroidered with the name of the temple they represent, or the names of their troupes. On the banners, there are very magnificent embroideries made out of golden and silver strings, as well as double dragons worshiping the pagoda in three-dimensional pattern. The middle part is left for the names of each temple or troupes. (photos 1, 2)

- 刺繡品上的紋飾多為吉祥圖案。金龍是尊貴吉祥的代表；魚是生活富足、有餘的祈福意涵；纏枝紋則有生生不息、子孫繁茂的寓意。（圖3）
  Auspicious patterns are most often seen patterns in the embroideries. Golden dragon is a symbol of nobility and good luck; and fish plentiful and surplus. The winding branch patterns imply glorious continuation of the clans. (photo 3)

糊紙

糊紙又稱紙紮，是以紙（棉紙、彩紙、油紙、玻璃紙）與竹篾條為主要材料所製成。使用於歲時祭儀、生命禮儀以及喪禮祭祀的場合，例如：建醮、王船祭典、做十六歲、賀壽、送靈等。糊紙成品有許多種類，其中又以花燈、風箏、七娘媽亭、壽庭、神偶、大士爺、龍鳳亭、王船、紙厝等為最多見。

PAPER-PASTING

Paper-pasting is also called paper binding, meaning making different articles by using paper (rice paper, color paper, grease paper and cellophane) and bamboo strips. It is necessary in festivals, ceremonies, funeral rituals, for example, the occasions like Cheung Chau (Taoist Festival of Peace and Renewal), Ship Deity worshipping, Adulthood Ceremony (attaining manhood at the age of sixteen), birthday, funerals and so forth. There are different forms of paper-pasting, such as lanterns, kites, Seven Sisters' pavilion, divine figures, Da Shu Ye (the leader of ghost), dragon and phoenix pavilion, ships of the Ship Deity and house for the dead.

- 糊紙的製作，首先劈竹枝做出骨架，用棉線細綁竹枝，繼而剪裁合適的紙張，先糊底紙撐起形體，紙面上再貼上彩紙剪貼的字畫即完成。（圖1-4）

  The first step of paper-pasting is to cut bamboo sticks into slender strips and tie them as the frames with cotton strings. After the paper is cut proper size, the primary paper is pasted to form the body, and to finish by pasting colorful patterns and cutting-out phrases and images. (photos 1-4)

- 靈厝是為燒化給往生者所製作。它可說是一間應有盡有的理想住所，形式與內容均可由主家訂製時選定，可以是傳統住屋、亭台樓閣或豪華洋樓、甚至是一座宮殿。（圖5）

  Ling Tsuo is a paper-pasted house for the dead in a funeral ceremony. It is almost an perfect mansion with whatever one would expect to have in his lifetime. The style and belongings are decided by the purchaser, whether traditional estate with pavilions or Western mansion, even a royal palace. (photo 5)

• 在建醮、普渡的場合，可見到立於壇場外的紙糊神像。其中，大士爺（圖1）是統治諸鬼的鬼王，青面獠牙、口吐火舌；頭頂則嵌有收服祂的觀世音菩薩、綠度母或摩訶迦羅神像。山神（圖2）則常與土地公並列在壇場兩側。

During the ceremonies of Cheung Chau, Pu Du (sending the ghosts to reincarnation during the Ghost Festival), one can see all kinds of paper-pasted divine statues around the altars. Da Shu Ye (photo 1) is the one who governs the ghosts, and on top his head, there are the statue of Guan Yin (Bodhisattva), Green Tara or Mahakala. Da Shu Ye is modeled as green-faced, protruding teeth, flaming from his mouth. The God of the Mountains (photo 2) and the God of the Land are usually on each side of the altar.

• 紙糊的侍祭成品在普渡結束後，都要點火焚化。主持的道士誦經作法、普渡亡魂後，將紙糊神像、紙厝、金銀山焚化，火光熊熊，整個儀式於是完成。（圖3）

All the paper-pasted articles are brunt after Pu Du. The hosting Taoist priests chant and practice magic to sending the ghosts to reincarnation and set fire to the paper statues, houses, gold and silver mountains to complete the rituals. (photo 3)

3

打鐵仔店

在農業社會裡，所有生產用的鐵製工具，都是靠打鐵舖供應，因而打鐵店就在地方上聚集形成「打鐵仔街」。以手工打造的鐵器刀具，與一般大量生產的刀具相比，差別就在於手工製造出來的是「鐵包鋼」，外面兩層是鐵，中間一層是鋼，鋼使刀口堅硬銳利、不易崩裂、捲口。

FORGE

In the agricultural period, all the iron devices were provided by the blacksmith, and very often, all the forgers would gather in one area of the town and from a forge ghetto. The hand-made iron devices and knives are different from the mass productions with its "steal wrapped by iron" feature, as in a knife, the two sides are iron, and the blade in between is steal-made, so to reinforce the sharpness and prevent the blade from crumbling or curling.

- 打鐵的工夫，在於用眼睛觀察火色，打鐵要趁熱。製作者需依照刀具種類選擇鐵材，並反覆燒紅、退火、錘打鐵塊而逐漸成形。（圖1-2）
  The secrets of forge is about observing the flame and forging while the temperature is right. The smiths select raw materials according to the categories of knives to be made. The iron is repeatedly heated up and forged and cooled, until the burning iron is formed to desired shape. (photos 1-2)

- 農業機械化之後，手工製作的農具需求量減少許多，因而打鐵店舖在零星製作特定的鋤、犁具及各式刀、鑿、剪類之外，多半同時兼營其他生意。（圖3）
  After the agriculture is industrialized, the demand of hand-made farm implements dropped, and then forges transferred to small productions, such as hoes, ploughs and other knives, chisels, and scissors, and the blacksmiths usually need to combine other business with forging. (photo 3)

蒸籠

竹木香、糯米香，是與年節喜慶相連在一起的氣味。以桂竹片、亞杉木片所製成的蒸籠，為台灣人蒸煮出食物的自然風味以及恰如其分的口感質地。蒸籠的製作，秘訣在於刀法和力道，製作者必須運用純熟的技巧來刨削竹片，編成蒸盤底，並用木片圍成邊框，才能完成。

STEAMER

The Lunar New Year and other festivals are often glorified by the fragrance of bamboo and wood, and the sweet smell of glutinous rice. The steamers made of bamboo and fir most properly work up the natural flavor and taste the best. The key to streamer producing is the mastering of the knife and the operator's strength. He has to pare and plan the bamboo strips painstakingly with excellent skills and weave the strips as the bottom and circle the wood to form the wall.

• 製作蒸籠時，司傅先以噴了水的木片圍成外框，削出錯口，並以藤蕊紮緊；在第一層外框的內緣還要再卡上一層，並以木夾夾緊。這就需要一些力氣和足夠的技巧。（圖1）

When making a streamer, the workman puts the wetted wood blocks together in a circular shape and make cuts for fastening rattan strings; after adding another layer in the inside of the first layer, the streamer is temporarily fixed with wooden clamps. This would require some strength and sufficient skills. (photo 1)

• 蒸籠的製作過程包括：剖竹、選材、拗木（圖2）、固定（圖3）、加厚、做底（圖4）、做蓋（圖5,6）、做耳（圖7）。

The process of making a streamer by sequence are ripping open the bamboo, selecting wood, bending the wood into shape (photo 2), fixing (photo 3), thickening the layers, weaving the bottom sieve-like bottom (photo 4), making the cover (photos 5, 6), and finish with the completion of the ears. (photo 7)

燈籠

燈籠是結合編竹、糊裱與彩繪，可以透光的工藝品。高掛的燈籠，象徵照路、吉祥與光明。彩繪的圖樣、字體與色彩，是製作的司傅主要承繼傳統、揮灑創意的重點。形制上，橢圓的瓜形與圓筒形是最基本的樣式。

LANTERN

A lantern is a illuminating handicrafts of the combination of weaving bamboo strips, paper pasting and color painting. The lanterns hanging high symbolize guiding the way, auspicious blessings and bright perspective. The patterns of color paintings, fonts and colors are where the artist can bring his talents into full play. The long oval-shaped melon and round tube-shape lanterns are most constantly seen.

1

- 彩繪和書寫文字是製作過程中技巧與美感最高的部份；在圓筒形燈籠的表面繪製，需要精確的控制比例、線條，比平面繪製的難度要高許多。（圖1）
  Color painting and calligraphy on the lanterns require the artist's critical skills and highly aesthetic sense. While painting on the tube-shaped lantern, the controlling of accuracies of the proportions and line is much difficult than painting on a flat surface. (photo 1)

- 燈籠透出的溫暖、昏黃的燈光，配上吉慶的大紅字體，使得整個廟內的空間益增溫馨與古色古香。（圖2）
  The warmth and faint light emitting from the lanterns, plus the big red delightful written characters, make the temple a cozy and comfortable place, as well as the archaic air. (photo 2)

1

• 十二生肖是花燈常見的主題，輪到馬年就會有許多以駿馬為主題，如馬到成功、一馬當先、馬上封侯的花燈。（圖1）

The twelve Chinese zodiac signs play the leading role in the lanterns. When turning into the Year of Horse, one can see in various occasions the lanterns with the horse themes, such as "Gaining the success as the horse arrives" (to get immediate success), "As fast as the fasted horse" (to take the lead) and "Being granted as an official on the horse back" (to win success in the officialdom). (photo 1)

• 廟宇內外所懸掛的傘燈，可寫上廟名或奉祀的主神名號。字體一般用朱紅色的明體或宋體字，有一定的筆畫順序、粗細和間架配置關係。（圖2）

The umbrella lanterns are hanging around the temples and the names of the temple and the major god are written on the lanterns. The fonts of red Ming and Sung are used, following certain stroke sequences, thickness and layout. (photo 2)

• 婚、喪、喜、慶等不同用途的燈籠，各有固定形制，不能混用。喜慶用的燈（圖3,4,6）用於商店開幕或年節張掛。兩姓合婚燈（圖5）使用於婚禮，雙方家裡各置一對。字姓燈（圖7）用於宗祠或民宅的祖先廳、大廳，代表崇祖、正本清源並祈求人丁興旺。

Various types of lanterns are made for different purposes. They are made according to a unchanged system, and can not allowed to be misused. For example, the lanterns for joyous events (photos 3, 4, 6) are used in grand opening or festivals around the year. The wedding lanterns (photo 5) are only used in the weeding and it requires the bride and the groom to hang a pair of them in each of their own families. Clan lanterns (with the family name and the name of origination descent are written on them) are hung in the ancestral halls or the hall of ordinary residence. It serves as a symbol of remembering the ancestors and the origination, as well as a prayer for a growing family. (photo 7)

舞蹈之美

The
Beauty of Dance

舞蹈之美

撰文◎趙綺芳　東華大學民族文化學系助理教授

台灣原住民具有十分獨特的舞蹈文化。原住民各族群在島上各自有其獨立的文化體系，以豐富的口傳文學與祭儀文化，傳承族群的集體心靈圖像，包含對人與自然關係的辨思、對宇宙的敬畏、維繫社群生存與秩序的企圖等等。

人類透過肢體的律動，來表達無法言喻的悸動或情感，其歷史可追溯自語言發生之前。不同人群經年累月地經由肢體創作的傳承與創新，形成可供辨識的族群符號體系，因此，台灣原住民各族的舞蹈各有特色，且與社會規範與文化意涵緊密結合。

在台灣原住民各族之中，阿美族發展出較為顯著的舞蹈文化。舉凡重要的年中祭儀，或是族人的社會聚集，如婚禮、家屋落成、從軍或是學成歸鄉等慶祝場合，皆可見族人吟歌起舞。其祭儀舞蹈形式往往遵循各部落的傳統，嚴謹而不可任意變動。男性依照年齡階級層規範，長幼有序地持續在艷陽下齊聲高歌、奮力躍動；這些文化定義下的專業舞者，透過身體展現部落團結精神。類似的祭儀舞蹈象徵與意義，亦可見諸鄰近的卑南族所舉行的「大獵祭」。

達悟族的小米舞。
The millet dance of the Tao people.

北鄒的mayasvi，或譯作「團結祭」，每年固定於達邦與特富野兩社舉行。祭儀歌舞以男性為主體，結合對天神的敬仰，在神聖的迎神與送神曲之間，一連串的群體歷史與豐收祈願歌謠，貫穿儀式。舞者的莊嚴律動，傳達出對天神的敬崇與謙卑俯伏的心情。

而對台灣本島人口最少的原住民族──賽夏族──而言，祭儀舞蹈的形式與風格，截然不同於前述；其意義必須透過「矮人祭」（pasta'ay）的文化情境予以理解。處於群強環伺下的賽夏族人，唯有祭儀中能悠悠吟誦交纏著先人悔恨與矮人告誡的樂音，反覆的舞步、前後擺動的肢體律動與忽前忽後的隊形，顯現了牽動族群集體命運的張力。

排灣與魯凱兩族，在五年祭與貴族婚禮中常見盛大舞隊，簡單的四步舞，維繫傳統價值的樸素與莊重。在沉緩的舞蹈行進間，根源於貴族社會的階級與性別意識清晰可見，一種富含秩序的美感油然而生。

位居蘭嶼的達悟族，或見男性瞠目以顫動的肢體斥退惡靈，或見女性以身體和頭髮的律動呼應海洋的波動，充分表達人和自然間純然無矯飾的溝通。

至於被認為沒有「舞蹈」概念與表現的布農族，和文化變遷最徹底以致傳統舞蹈脈絡難尋的泰雅族與邵族，以及目前正熱烈尋求正名的平埔族等，在現代化與追尋認同的過程中，逐漸塑模出群體的律動符號體系，其舞步與動作或許簡單，心情卻是複雜。

而在台灣原住民的舞蹈體系中，每一種簡單的舞步背後，都有一整套深層的文化意涵：是一個綿延的人群，經由多年的歷史沉澱，所堆砌而成的意義與形式體系，其價值與美感，往往不是華麗與精緻的，而是質樸卻深沉的。

The Beauty of Dance

Text: Chao Chi-fang   Assistant Prof., Department of Indigenous Cultures, National Dong Hwa University

The Dance cultures of the Aboriginal peoples in Taiwan are very unique. The Aboriginal peoples on this island have independent cultural systems of their own, and rich oral literature and rituals are used to hand down each of their own community spiritual recognitions, including the relationship between human being and the nature, the awe to the universe, and the continuation of clan surviving and orderly ambitions.

Human beings, through the rhythm of the body, express nondescript emotional throb, and such a history can be traced back the time before language was developed. Different people, in ineffable long period of time, and by means of heritages and creation by the body, originated an identical symbol system of the very clan, therefore, the dances of the Aboriginal peoples in Taiwan are uniquely characterized, and intimately connected to the social norm and cultural significance.

Among the Aboriginal peoples, Amis tribe developed more outranking form of dance culture than the others. It is easy to spot the tribesmen singing and dancing, whenever there are annual rituals, or social getting-together for various celebrations, such as weeding, completion of new houses, enlisting in the military service, returning home after finishing education and etc. The ritual dances are restricted by each tribe's tradition, and is firmly unchangeable. The males, according to their age levels, orderly singing, dancing and jumping athletically under the high sun; and after the dance, these culturally defined professional dancers have shown the united spirit of the tribe. The symbol and meaning of such a ritual dance and the similar can also be seen in adjacent Puyuma Tribe's "Grand Hunting Ritual."

The word "mayasvi" of Northen Tsou tribe means Ritual of Being United, and it is held in certain date in Da-bang Hosa and Te-fu-ye Hosa. The males are the body of the ritual singing and dancing. Combing the worship to god, the sacred welcome and farewell songs of welcoming gods and a succession of song on tribal history and harvest praying, singing and dances pass through the rituals. The dancers' solemn movement have expressed humbly their reverence to the gods.

The Saixia has the least population among the tribes, and their ritual dance is greatly different from that of the others. Its meaning is only understood through pasta'ay (Pygmies Ceramony). Surrounded by the powerful neighbors, Saixia's power that effects the community destiny is strengthened when they sing and recite the songs that entangles with their ancestor's regrets and the warning of the pygmies, and when they repeatedly dance, swing back and forth and the occurrence of the array's sudden forward and backward.

Paiwan and Rukai run very stately dance in their Five Year Festival and noble weddings. Simple four step dance holds together the modesty and solemnity of their traditional values. During the slow and grave dance, the crucial distinction of social rank and gender that derived from aristocrat system and it sense of order are clearly seen.

When Tao tribe, living in Orchid Island, dance, the males open their eyes wide and with trembling body to expel the evil force, and the females uniquely respond to the undulation of the ocean with their body movement and long cascaded hair flinging and the unaffected communication between human and the nature is made.

As to Bunun tribe that is identified as tribe without dance, and Taiya tribe and Thao tribe that experienced so severe cultural change that the origin of their dances can never be traced again, and the Pingpu Tribe that now eagerly to regain their tribal name, are all in a modernizing and pursuing identity stage, and eventually molding their own moving symbol system. Their dance and movement maybe simple, but their feelings are mixed.

Behind each simple dance step of the Aboriginal peoples, there's a complete set of significant cultural meaning; it is a system of import and forms stacked by long period's depositing and the value and beauty are seldom splendid and intricate, but austere and profound.

● 達悟族男性在祭儀舞蹈中較少牽起手跳舞，然而其動作力度美感十足。
  Tao's men seldom dance hand in hand in their rituals, however, the
  movements are intensively beautiful.

2

- 年祭中的舞蹈對阿美族男性而言，是最佳體能訓練。（圖1）
  The dances in annual rituals are the best physical training to the Amis. (photo 1)

- 達悟族女性身著藍白相間條紋的傳統服飾跳舞；在達悟族舞蹈中鮮少有異性同舞的情形。（圖2）
  Tao women dance vigorously, wearing traditional blue and white strip dress. Tao women and men rarely dance together. (photo 2)

• 鄒族的團結祭是以男性為主體的祭儀，舞蹈隊形多以半圓形呈現，動作凝練莊重。（圖1）
The mayasvi of Tsuo people is limited to man. The dance team usually array semi-circularly, and their movement can be very solemn. (photo 1)

• 阿美族的傳統舞蹈動作中有海洋文化的元素，例如靈巧的隊形和俐落的騰躍動作。（圖2）
The traditional Amis dance contains oceanic flavor, such as indigenous formation and well-executed curvet movement. (photo 2)

• 矮靈祭中，賽夏族人以螺旋形的開合為隊形，伴著背後的臀鈴起舞。（圖3）
During pasta'ay, the Saixia firstly array their teams in spiral shape, and dance with accompany of their small buttocks bells. (photo 3)

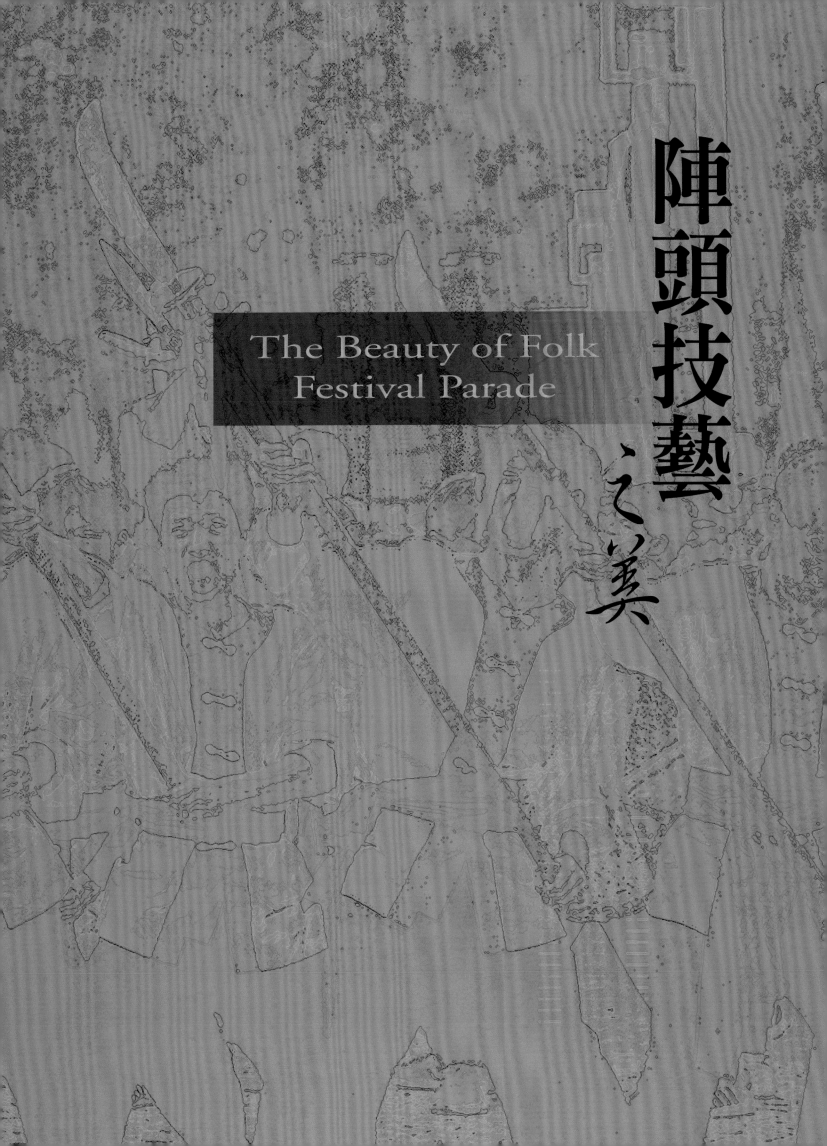

陣頭技藝
之美

The Beauty of Folk
Festival Parade

陣頭技藝之美

審定◎江韶瑩　國立台北藝術大學傳統藝術研究所所長
撰文◎陳怡方　國立台北藝術大學傳統藝術研究所碩士

在台灣民間社會中，民間信仰具有十分強大的無形力量。特別是地方大廟舉辦神誕、平安祭、建醮或普渡時，通常能讓當地角頭社團、老少全部投入其中。在這樣的熱鬧廟會場合中，最吸引人的就是跟隨在神轎前後一支支爭奇鬥豔的彩旗、轎班、表演隊伍。他們的裝扮與儀仗排場繽紛炫目，激昂的鼓吹樂和陣式變化，充滿震懾全場的神秘力量，有時也會以逗趣的演出使人駐足。這些以民間廟會為表演舞台的行列，便是「陣頭」。

陣頭伴隨神明出巡、遶境、暗訪或進香活動而來。主廟的神明外出巡視其轄境稱為遶境，主要目的是宣揚神威與驅逐境內邪祟、除疫防煞；沿途接受信眾的膜拜，將靈力分予信眾並為信眾祈福。參與遊街的陣頭，一方面有為神明座前護駕的意思，另一方面也為慶典活動帶來熱鬧歡愉的氣氛；既展現對神明最虔誠的敬意，也為人們帶來生活中的娛樂。

陣頭的種類眾多，學者將其分成「雜技」與「小戲」兩種，各自有其淵源與發展，然而都在廟會、節慶時出陣。「雜技」陣頭演出需要有良好的合作默契、技術與充沛的體力，其起源和宗教祭祀、勞動遊戲、護衛戰爭有關。「小戲」的稱呼則是相對於登上舞台演出的「大戲」而言，是由農村的人們或民間藝人所創作而流傳的小型歌舞、戲曲。藉著即興編造的對白與歌詞，演出民間的生活百態和感情。

雜技性質的陣頭有：舞獅、高蹺陣、布馬陣、跳鼓陣、鬥牛陣、宋江陣、金獅陣、白鶴陣等活動力大、有武打味道的「武陣」，平常藉練習來健身。小戲性質的陣頭包括：車鼓陣、採茶戲、竹馬陣、牛犁陣、跑旱船、素蘭陣等等，是歌舞較多、娛樂的成分較高的「文陣」。此外，還有民間曲館擔綱演出的南、北管子弟團以及宗教性極強的藝閣、八家將、官將首和神將團等。隨著民間社會的變動，陣頭演出的種類和形式亦隨之增多，老的陣頭消失或創新改良，新的陣頭也不斷冒出。原先農閒時由在地社區自行組成的業餘陣頭，在「輸人不輸陣」的心理下，平時即積極排練；而職業性陣頭則遊走於全台各地廟會。

扮相特異的將爺陣。
The divine generals with particular dress and make-up.

台灣的陣頭，其步調與民間信仰、廟會節慶及地方上的年中行事相一致。在一代一代的生活裡，踏步於大街廣場的陣頭，早已是這塊土地上人民生活的深刻樣貌。敲響鑼鼓，吹起號角，出陣在即，陣頭裡的人們個個如有神在。在濃妝、面具之下，他們有的是最具活動力的青少年，然而更多的是一般人難以想像的中壯、老人，他們出陣之際，虎虎生風益勝少年郎。目睹此景，陣頭的力量不難想像。

The Beauty of Folk Festival Parade

Supervision: Chiang Shao-ying — Director, Graduate School of Folk Culture & Arts, Taipei National University of the Arts

Text: Chen Yi-fang — MA, Graduate School of Folk Culture & Arts, Taipei National University of the Arts

The power of folk beliefs are tremendous and, however, invisibly mighty in Taiwanese daily life. Whenever there are feast for feeding hungry ghosts and comfort the wandering souls during the Ghost Festival, and the Taoist Festival of Peace and Renewal, it often inspires all the people of the society, old and young, male and female, with glamorous banners and palanquin processions and performer of all sorts into action and impels them to be as devoting as they can. In all the temple fairs, the most fascinating phenomenon is those colorful and glamorous parades that follow the patron gods making rounds of their territories. The parades, shining in costumes and dazzling in paraphernalia, when performing, would either emit unspeakable mysterious power or awesomely entertaining attractions that captivate and charm the hearts of the audience. This is the Folk Festival Parades, staged in temple fairs, and the most essential way to worship gods.

The Folk Festival Parades are organized for escorting the patron gods, while they make rounds and inspecting each of their patronized areas and advocate their deity exploits, as well as dispelling the evil power out of their divine jurisdictions, they at the same time embrace the worship from their believers and, in return, distribute the divine might and blessing to them. The Folk Festival Parades, while being the patron gods' escorting guards, perform the best they can to make the events colorful and joyous. It doesn't just unfold their most pious respect and honor to gods, but also entertain the ordinary people with gustoes and delights.

There are various kinds of Divine Parades. In general, the scholars of the field divide it into two major categories: Variety Performances parades and Mimic Drama parades. As the terms indicate, a variety performance is related to acrobatic and physical activity that requires excellent techniques, physical strength and cooperation, and is derived from laborious works, games, religious rituals, and even wars, while Mimic Drama is an imitation of drama acted on formal stages, and is performed by folk artist or farmers, or people from all trades, completed with impromptu dialogue and songs to express different lifestyles and spiritual value.

The Variety Performance parades include the martial formation such as Lion Puppet Dance, Stilts-walking, comic Cloth-horse Performance, the Jumping Drums, imitative Bull Fight, Sung-Jiang formation, Golden Lion formation, White Crane formation and other fitness-wise activities. In the meantime, the more recreational, entertaining and non-martial Mimic Drama parades are consisted of Cart Drum formation, Plough Dance, Running Dry Boat, Picking-tea-leaves Operas, Su Lan formation and so forth. What is more, there are folk musical groups such as Nankuan and Peikuan performances, and more religious Eight Generals, the decorated Towers, God Commands, God General Troupe and so forth. Following the ever changing social trends, those formations transformed, too. Some old formations have cloistered into mere memories, but some, or even more, new formations at the same time have come with the tide of fashion. The amateur formations, once were organized by farmers and practiced in leisure time. Nowadays they are formed by local community members and are vigorous participators of such activities in each community. On the contrary, the professional formations perform island-wide, wherever there are temple fairs.

Taiwan's Folk Parades and folk beliefs, temple fairs and local calendar are synchronized. The artistry advances at the same time with the development of the people. Generations after generations, being a role in such parades, however significant or insignificant it can be, has been so essential to the people. They emerge into the parades, as the gongs hit and drums beaten, and as the horn blown to sign the setting-out. Under their heavy make-up and fascinating masks, there are not just the putative vigorous youths, but, surprisingly, more elderly people who are even more energetic then the youths. For all these, the attraction, significance, and power of the festival parades have told its own tale.

● 涼傘舞動，帶起廟會的熱鬧氣氛。
As the canopies swirl, the joyous temple fair is initiated.

家將團

台灣專司地方平靖的神祇，大都
有其「人間部將」，監察善惡、
除魔捉妖，這就是廟會陣頭的
「家將團」。一般多以八人為制，
所以也稱「八家將」。實際上，
家將團從四人到十八人都有。家
將團一般是指甘、柳、謝、范四
將，加上春、夏、秋、冬四爺；
另有文、武二差在前引路；還有
一人負責肩挑三十六種刑具。

ESCORTING GENERALS

Escorting Generals are the subjected to
the patron gods, and are entitled to elim-
inate the evil spirits and seize the wicked.
They are generally called Escorting Generals, and are often seen in a group of
eight people, and this is also the name of
Eight Generals was from. As a matter of
fact, each Escorting Generals group can
be formed by four to eighteen members. Usually, the generals indicate General Gan, Liu, Shieh, and Fan, plus the
four generals of spring, summer, autumn
and winter, and civil and martial officials,
and the one who carries thirty-six instruments of torture.

- 畫臉師傅按各將之性格、職司畫好臉譜之
  後，才能接領神令出巡；臉譜圖案則視各
  團畫師之特色與習慣而不同。（圖1-4）
  The faces of the generals are painted dif-
  ferently according to their personalities
  and responsibilities. They are allowed to
  take divine orders only after the make-up
  is completed. The make-up patterns vary,
  depending on each artist's preference and
  talents. (photos 1-4)

- 家將團成員被畫上臉譜之後，會再進行開
  光、上馬儀式，此後扮演者即為家將神的
  化身，必須戒慎恐懼，不得嘻笑怒罵。
  「禁口不語」是出陣時的首要禁忌。
  （右圖）
  After facial make-up is completed, the
  God Generals go through initiation and
  horse granting ceremonies. They are pro-
  hibited to talk, for now, they are divine
  characters. Making jokes, laughter and
  any personal emotional reaction is restrict-
  edly forbidden. Keep silence is the first
  taboo to obey while in a parade.
  (photo, right)

- 家將除了驅逐邪祟、捉拿鬼魅外，尚有解運祈安、安宅鎮煞及維持秩序等功能，圖1是搭七星橋，助信眾改運求平安，圖2是喪禮出軍的家將。（圖1-2）
The Escorting Generals take charge of driving off the evil force, catching the wicked spirits, releasing one's bad luck, giving blessing, oppress the malignant deities and keep order of the spiritual world and so on. Photo 1 shows the Seven Star Bridge helping people to get rid of bad luck. Photo 2 shows that Escorting Generals attend the funerals.

- 家將出陣時的步法與陣法架勢十足。家將擺出七星步、四門陣、八卦陣等陣法，攻擊並圍捕鬼魅邪祟，以求安民保境。陣法擺開之後，閒人不得入陣，以避免沖煞或發生肢體碰撞的危險。（圖3）
The formations for the God Generals are powerful. The Seven Star Steps, Four Gate Array and Eight Diagrams Array are applied when attacking and bust evil spirits, so to protect people and the regions. When the arrays are settled, irrelevant people are not allowed to go in, a way to prevent spiritual impact or physical collision. (photo 3)

十二婆姐

「婆姐」原是協助臨水夫人陳靖姑來保護孩童健康成長的神明。婆姐本有三十六位，一般僅以前十二位為陣頭成員，因此稱為「十二婆姐」，過去都由男性扮演。除婆姐外，陣中還有「婆姐媽」與「婆姐囝仔」兩種角色。行進間或表演時，都是由十二婆姐之首的陳大娘領陣，成排緩步而優雅地演出，但婆姐媽與婆姐囝仔的行動卻忽前忽後，完全不受限制。

THE TWELVE NURSING GODDESSES

The Nursing Goddesses were helpers of Lady Lin-sui, Chen Jing gu, to protect children and nurse their health. Originally, there were thirty-six Nursing Goddesses, however, due to mostly only twelve of them attend the parades, they are called the Twelve Nursing Goddesses. Except their presence, one usually can see Granny Goddesses and Granny's Children. When in procession, they are led by Nursing Goddess Chen, the leader of the group. The Nursing Goddesses all gracefully walk in neat arrays, while, Granny Goddesses and Granny's Children can run around as they wish.

- 十二婆姐通常臉戴面具，身著大紅的鳳仙裝、五彩霞披，左手持陽傘，右手拿扇。一路踩著小碎步，搖搖擺擺的走著，俗豔又帶喜氣。（圖1）
The Nursing Goddesses, in red garden balsam style suits (fen sien zuang), and with their face masked and umbrellas in their left hands, fans in the right, walk in very short span and sway all the way. They are flamboyant and full of joy. (photo 1)

- 婆姐媽穿著藍色婦裝，肩扛黑傘，手執枴杖，沿路照顧四處尋母的婆姐囝仔。婆姐囝仔在陣中來回穿梭，一個亂跑一個追趕，扮演串場的逗趣角色。（圖2-4）
The Granny Goddesses, dressed in blue, black umbrellas on their shoulders and walking stick in their hands, all the way take care of those Granny's Children who in the parades symbolize lost kids looking for their mothers. They, all together, swiftly shuttle between procession like mimics, and often make the audience burst into laughter. (photos 2-4)

舞獅

舞獅，又稱「弄獅」。它的組成是一人舞獅頭、一人弄獅尾，在前面另有一「獅鬼」執葵扇弄獅。以新竹為界，台灣南部為閉口獅，北部為開口獅，另有醒獅（廣東獅）、北方獅（北京獅）。昔日舞獅有辟邪驅祟及娛樂健身的功能。現在除廟會之外，一般的晚會、開幕、選舉等場合，都有機會看見舞獅。

LION PUPPET DANCING

The Lion Puppet Dancing, usually called "teasing the lions", are consisted of three people. One supports the lion head, and the other the rear part and tail. The third one is called "lion ghost", with a palm-leaf fan in hand, teasing the lion. Shinchu County is the boundary of two major Lion Puppet Dancing forms; to the south, namely close-mouthed lions , and to the north, open-mouthed lions. There are also Guangdong lion dancing and Beijing lion dancing. In the old time, lions in Lion Puppet Dancing functioned as auspicious beast to dispel evil forces, as well as a way of physical exercise and entertaining.

- 「醒獅」除舞獅外，還有特技演出。它的特色表演是「採青」，原意來自昔日過年時在門口放青菜，引瑞獅咬取以求福氣；現代則成為「咬紅包」特技。（圖1,2）
  Guangdong lion dancing, aside from its lion teasing session, there are stunt shows. It is characterized with catching the greens, referring in the old time that, during Chinese New Year, people would place green vegetables in their doorsteps and asked the lions to catch with their mouths, as a symbol of requesting luck. However, as a new custom, the vegetables are replaced by red envelop, with money inside. (photos 1, 2)

- 獅頭的造型各異，閉口獅的獅嘴固定不能隨意開啟，開口獅的獅嘴可以上下活動。舞獅的動作常模仿真獅，轉身扭頭、滾地趴睡，生動逗趣，更添廟會的歡慶氣氛。（圖3-6）
  A lion's head is the most intricate part of the whole structure. Usually, the mouth of a close-mouthed lion is fixed, while the mouth of an open-mouthed lion is able to move with its jaw. The action of Lion Puppet Dancing is very plausible, no matter turning the body around or move the head are all very vivid, indeed a must for the joyous celebrations in the temple fairs. (photos 3-6)

1

高蹺陣

高蹺陣的表演者需踩上三尺左右的木蹺，做高度技巧的演出。高蹺可分為「文高蹺」與「武高蹺」。前者著重人物表情與情節表演，動作細膩、唱工講究，有台詞和劇情；後者以特技或打拳為主，台灣各地的高蹺陣多屬此類。但各地亦有不同特色，南部多打拳、耍兵器；中部多雜耍、翻觔斗；北部為弄獅、單腳跳、七尺高蹺。

STILT-WALKING

The stilts in Stilt-Walking can be as high as one meter, and the artists would perform very skillful presentations. Stilt-Walking are put into two categories: Gentle Stilt-Walking and Martial Stilt-Walking, the former emphasize facial expression and plots, mostly with intricate gesture and singing, and the songs and stories are often very touching; the latter mostly focus on stunt and Chinese boxing, it is also the most commonly seen in Taiwanese Stilt-Walking performance. However, each area has its own distinctive characteristics, among the examples, Stilt-Walking in Southern Taiwan features boxing and weapon performing; Middle Taiwan, variety shows and acrobatic somersaults; while the North is mostly familiar with teasing lion puppets, single-foot jump and two-meter high stilt-walking.

• 高蹺陣常演出的戲碼有「關公保二嫂」、「拾玉鐲」、「潘金蓮挑簾子」等。一般的遊行隊伍則以「三藏取經」、「八仙過海」等化妝表演為主。高蹺陣沒有一定的人數，七、八人或十多人都可，獨演或會演皆可。（圖1-6）
The stories of Stilt-Walking include Lord Gwan Escorting and Protecting His Second Sister-in-law, Picking Jade Bracelet, Pan Jin Lian Raises the Curtain and so on; however, when in procession form, one mostly can see Tang San Zuan Goes on A Pilgrimage for Buddhist Scriptures, Eight Fairies Compete with Each Other While Crossing the Sea and other themes that emphasize in make-up and costumes. A Stilt-Walking team usually is consisted of seven to eight people, but sometimes might up to more than ten people. They either perform alone or in group, depending on the stories. (photos 1-6)

4

5

6

竹馬陣

竹馬陣，是以十二生肖為表演型態的南管陣頭，表演有唱、舞和口白。十二生肖的扮像，最早是各依角色穿掛竹製道具，如同騎竹馬，所以稱為竹馬陣。竹馬陣由「老鼠頭」為首，帶領「十二生軍」（十二生肖）驅邪除穢、普救眾生。配合神明的威力與神咒，成員在傳統樂器的配樂和歌聲中，腳踏七星步，依序擺開不同的陣勢演出。

BAMBOO-HORSE FORMATION

The Bamboo-Horse Formation is primarily a Nankuan Opera performance, but the performers dress up and make up as the twelve characters in Chinese Horoscope. Originally, there were much clung to bamboo ornaments, for example, riding bamboo made horses, and that is where the name Bamboo-Horse Formation was from. Bamboo-Horse Formation is led by a Mouse Head, the first sign of Chinese Horoscope, and with its eleven followers, they drive away the evil forces and rescue people from disasters. They, accompanied by traditional music and songs, present Seven-Star Array different array steps and gesture to operate in coordination with god's power.

- 竹馬陣成員原來穿掛竹製道具演出，後因製作較為麻煩，便捨棄道具而以戲服象徵角色，共有五旦七生，各有兵器。（圖1-4）
The Bamboo-Horse Formation originally all equipped with bamboo-made properties, later, they was abandoned due to the difficulties of production, and were replaced with costumes. A Bamboo-Horse Formation is usually made up of five female and seven male characters, and armed with weapons. (photos 1-4)

- 老鼠頭（圖右藍衣者）一出場，先來點名，眾生肖便一一現身，各依自己的本性踩踏舞步，並且配上一段自我介紹的開場白。（圖5）
When the Mouse Head, the leader, dressed in blue in the picture, appears on the scene, he would call the roll first, and the rest eleven characters show up in sequence, and dance in a way according to what animal they present in the Chinese Horoscope, and give self-introductions. (photo 5)

神將

神將，是高約成人兩倍大小的神
像，由一人藏身於內，扛弄或舞
跳。其身形廣碩，高高在上，走
起路來左右搖晃，兩隻手大幅前
後緩慢擺動，在沿街猛烈鞭炮和
鑼鼓聲中，愈顯神威赫赫、震攝
人心，頗具戲劇性的效果。神將
主要流行在宜蘭、台北和台中大
甲等地，在遶境或進香活動中，
經常可見。南部的神將則有五毒
大神、十三太保、二十四司、十
三金甲等。

GOD GENERAL

God Generals are high as twice of an
average adult, hollow inside, and are
carried by people. The movements are
always either extraordinary exaggerating, or very stately. No matter what,
they often give dignified and mighty,
even frightening air, with their huge
arms swinging, and the theatrical effects
of fire works. God Generals are most
popular in Yilan, Taipei and Dajia (Tai-
chong), and they spear in most worshiping and divine inspecting occasions.
As to the South, the God Generals of
those gods, such as Wu Do Da Sheng,
Thirteen Tai Bao, Twenty-four Si and
Thirteen Jin Jia are constantly seen.

• 神將經常成隊出現，職司清除地方不靖、
驅除瘟疫蟲害，以保護稻作收成。圖為三
十六官將，個個著盔甲戰服、粉臉素面，
高大英挺、氣勢逼人。（右圖）
God Generals mostly appear in troupe,
in order to repel the evil force, protecting
the harvest and so on. The picture shows
thirty-six God General Troupe; each of
them is full armour, fair-faced, and tall,
solemn and powerful. (photo, right)

- 《封神榜》中的二郎神楊戩，額頂長有三星眼，相貌堂皇，是主要的神將之一。民間相信祂神通廣大，能洞察世事，為問事解厄之神。（圖1）
  The three-eyed Er-lang God Yang Jian, from the legend of Feng Shen Bang (Rewarding the Gods), is one of the major God Generals to be seen in temple fairs. It's confidently believed that he has great power and sees through the world's looming evil air, and he is able to solve disastrous problems for people. (photo 1)

- 城隍爺的部將謝必安（圖2,3,5）、范無救（圖4），俗稱七爺、八爺。一高一矮的強烈對照和特異扮相，令為非作歹之徒不敢正視。
  The God General of Chi Ye (photos 2, 3, 5) and Ba Ye (photo 4), one tall and the other short, are subjected to City God. They are said to conduct the dead the Hell before reincarnation, and they usually scare away those who are not righteous in mind.

• 鹿港地區在境內發生災厄時，會由主其事的角頭廟舉
行「暗訪」。王爺於深夜巡視境域時，隨行的神將在
黑夜中行進，更顯其駭人威勢。（圖1,2,右圖）
Whenever there's any disaster happens in Lu Gang,
the patron temple would hold "secret call-on". The
patron god makes around the town during the night,
and his God Generals, at the same time, march with
him to dispel the evil forces. The scene is often very
shocking. (photos 1, 2, right)

鼓陣

以「鼓」為樂器，並以之命名的陣頭，有鑼鼓陣、開路鼓、跳鼓陣等。「鑼鼓陣」由鼓、鈸和大鑼組成，通常配合其他陣頭或神轎做為出陣的配樂。「開路鼓」以開路為目的，其鼓為特大號的大鼓，因此又名「大鼓陣」。「跳鼓陣」以跳躍和擊鑼鼓為主要的型態，活動時以傘旗和背鼓者為中心，作出多樣的隊形變化，跳躍進退。

CART-DRUM ARRAY

Drums are the major instrument used in the Cart-Drum Array, and the formation gives the name to the parade. There are Leading Drum, Jumping Drum, Gong Drum arrays, according to their categories and the way they perform. The Gong Drums arrays are consisted of drums, cymbals and gongs, and are usually act as accompanying groups to other kinds of arrays and gods' palanquins. The Leading Drum array, clear by its name, does lead the way for the parades, meanwhile, due the extra large drums used, they are also called Big Drum Arrays. The Jumping Drum arrays feature the performers' vigorous jumping and beating the gongs and drums. The performers encircle the person who carries a drum on his back, and change their formations, by way of jumping, and moving forward or backward.

- 跳鼓陣的組成由頭旗在前導引，鼓居中為主角，涼傘穿梭串場，銅鑼則分居四角搭配。職業陣頭為增加可看性，會加入疊羅漢、仰腰咬錢等特技演出。（圖1,2）
The Jumping Drum array has a fixed formation: flags leading the way, followed by drum performers, and the gong performers are positioned in the four corners, as the canopy carriers shuttle around them freely. Some professional groups, for expressing the audiences, would have their tumblers to form human pyramids, or bend backward to snatch money with their mouths. (photos 1, 2)

- 開路鼓在行進中一定會在輪車上表演，震耳的鼓聲形成熱鬧的廟會氣氛。（圖3）
The Leading Drum arrays always perform in carts, and its thundering drumbeats often climax the temple fairs. (photo 3)

宋江陣

宋江陣是全台灣最大且最具聲勢的武術陣頭，主要流行於南部地區。一般認為，宋江陣與水滸傳的梁山泊好漢有關。陣頭具有開路解厄、驅邪鎮煞和維持秩序的功能。主要種類有男子宋江陣、女子宋江陣、兒童宋江陣，以及從宋江陣變化的金獅陣、白鶴陣等。陣法變化中的「八卦陣」，是宋江陣操演時所不可缺少的重要陣勢，具有驅邪避凶、降妖伏魔的功效。

SUNG-JIANG FORMATION

By the standards both of momentum and size, Sung-Jiang Formation is on top of other formations. It is most popular in Southern Taiwan. It is said that Sun-Jiang Formation is related to the heroes of Liang San Lake in the legendary novel, Sui Fu, the Water Margin. The formation, like most others, functions to dispel evil forces, drive away bad lucks and bring peace to the people. The major groups include male Sung-Jiang arrays, female Sung-Jiang arrays and children Sung-Jiang arrays, and the variations, such as Golden Lion and White Crane formations. To all the arrays, the Eight Diagrams Array is must for all to learn and perform, and people firmly believe that it can drive out the evil spirit and make the demons back away.

- 宋江陣有護庄、保轎、練武、強身、團結的功能。其組成人數有三十六、五十、七十二、一百零八人陣等，以三十六人陣為最普遍。（圖1）
  Sung-Jiang Formation are said to protect the town, to unite townsmen, and also a fitness-wise practice. Each Sung-Jiang array is usually composed of either thirty-six, fifty, seventy-two, or one hundred and eight people, and the thirty-six formation is most commonly seen. (photo 1)

- 兵器在宋江陣中是不可少的，陣頭成員皆持兵器。兵器上貼有平安符，以保佑操演時不因失誤而受傷。（圖2-5）
  Weaponry is a must to Sung-Jiang Formation. The weapons held by the performers are specially blessed and with peace charms attached on the bodies, so to prevent any accident during performing. (photos 2-5)

197

【圖片來源】 （數目為頁碼）

◎ 1, 10, 14右, 15左, 17, 21, 23, 26下, 30, 31, 32, 33, 34圖1, 38, 39圖2-4, 46, 47, 54, 55, 56-57, 60-65, 68, 70, 71, 80圖3, 88-91, 93圖3, 94, 97圖5, 101圖4, 102-110, 111圖2.4.6, 113, 114, 115圖2.3.5, 116, 121圖2.3.4, 122, 124圖1.2, 127-129, 136下, 137, 138, 140圖1-5, 141-145, 148圖1, 149圖2.3, 150-152, 154-157, 159, 162, 164, 167, 172上, 173, 177, 180-182, 183圖5.6, 188, 190圖1, 191圖4, 194圖1, 195圖3, 196/ 郭娟秋 攝影

◎ 2, 6, 12, 14左, 15右, 19, 42, 78, 79, 80圖2, 83, 93, 95圖4, 111圖3.5, 115圖4, 117-120, 124圖3, 125, 126, 140圖6, 146, 147, 149圖5, 158, 183圖2.3, 184, 185, 190圖2, 191圖5, 192, 193/ 賴君勝 攝影

◎ 4, 28, 37圖2.3, 176圖2.3, 183圖4, 187, 191圖3, 195圖2/ 黃崑謀 攝影

◎ 93圖2, 100, 101圖3/ 莊展鵬 攝影

◎ 101圖2/ 陳輝明 攝影

◎ 101圖5/ 周舜瑾 攝影

◎ 112圖1/ 徐偉斌 攝影

◎ 112圖2-6, 153, 179/ 王智平 攝影

◎ 8, 75, 80圖1, 82, 84, 85/呂錘寬 攝影；國立傳統藝術中心 提供

◎ 26上, 27, 34圖2.3.4, 35, 36, 37圖4, 40, 41, 44, 45, 48-53, 58, 66, 67, 69, 74上, 76, 98, 99, 130-133, 136上, 176圖1.4, 178, 186/ 國立傳統藝術中心 提供

◎ 39圖5/ 高雄市立歷史博物館 提供

◎ 163, 166, 169/ 廖泰基攝影工作室 提供

◎ 168/ 楊雅棠 攝影‧提供

Photo credits:

◎ 1, 10, 14 (right), 15 (left), 17, 21, 23, 26 (down), 30, 31, 32, 33, 34 (photo 1), 38, 39 (photos 2-4), 46, 47, 54, 55, 56-57, 60-65, 68, 70, 71, 80 (photo 3), 88-91, 93 (photo 3), 94, 97 (photo 5), 101 (photo 4), 102-110, 111 (photos 2, 4, .6), 113, 114, 115 (photos 2, 3, 5), 116, 121 (photos 2, 3, 4), 122, 124 (photos 1, 2), 127-129, 136 (down), 137, 138, 140 (photos 1-5), 141-145, 148 (photo 1), 149 (photos 2, 3), 150-152, 154-157, 159, 162, 164, 167, 172上, 173, 177, 180-182, 183 (photos 5, 6), 188, 190(photo 1), 191(photo 4), 194(photo 1), 195(photo 3), 196/ Kuo Chuan-chiu

◎ 2, 6, 12, 14 (left), 15 (right), 19, 42, 78, 79, 80 (photo 2), 83, 93, 95 (photo 4), 111 (photos 3, 5), 115 (photo 4), 117-120, 124 (photo 3), 125, 126, 140 (photo 6), 146, 147, 149 (photo 5), 158, 183 (photos 2, 3), 184, 185, 190(photo 2), 191(photo 5), 192, 193/ Lai Jyun-sheng

◎ 4, 28, 37 (photos 2, 3), 176(photos 2, 3), 183 (photo 4), 187, 191 (photo 3), 195 (photo 2)/ Huang Kun-mou

◎ 93 (photo 2), 100, 101 (photo 3)/ Chuang Zhan-peng

◎ 101 (photo 2)/ Chen Hui-ming

◎ 101 (photo 5)/ Chou Shun-jin

◎ 112 (photo 1)/ Shu Wei-bing

◎ 112 (photo 2-6), 153, 179/ Wang Chi-ping

◎ 8, 75, 80 (photo 1), 82, 84, 85/ photographed by Lu Chui-kuan, provided by National Center for Traditional Arts

◎ 26 (up), 27, 34 (photo 2, 3, 4), 35, 36, 37 (photo 4), 40, 41, 44, 45, 48-53, 58, 66, 67, 69, 74 (up), 76, 98, 99, 130-133, 136 (up), 176 (photo 1, 4), 178, 186/ provided by National Center for Traditional Arts

◎ 39 (photo 5)/ provided by Kaohsiung Museum of History

◎ 163, 166, 169/ provided by Liao Tai Ji Photo Studio

◎ 168/ photographed and provided by Yang Ya-tang

台灣傳統藝術之美
The Beauty of Traditional Arts in Taiwan

指導機關／行政院文化建設委員會
出版者／國立傳統藝術中心
發行人／柯基良
地址／宜蘭縣五結鄉季新村五濱路二段201號
策劃／方芷絮、陳金泉
執行／黃素貞、邱建發、林建華
電話／(03) 960-5230　傳眞／(03) 960-5237
網址：www.ncfta.gov.tw　E-MAIL: ncfta@ms19.hinet.net

編輯製作／遠流出版事業股份有限公司　台灣館
地址／台北市南昌路二段81號6樓
電話／(02)2392-6899　傳眞／(02)2392-6658　郵撥／0189456-1
輸出印刷／中原造像股份有限公司

審定／汪志勇　呂錘寬　林會承　江韶瑩
撰文／鄭溪和　鄭昭民　陳怡方　趙綺芳
英文翻譯／鄭明華
專案攝影／郭娟秋
圖片提供／遠流台灣館　國立傳統藝術中心
　　　　　高雄市立歷史博物館　廖泰基攝影工作室　楊雅棠

主編／王明雪
執行編輯／吳梅瑛
美術編輯／郭倖惠
美術統籌／黃崑謀

出版日期／2003年12月30日　初版一刷
定價／新台幣1500元
著作權顧問／蕭雄淋律師
法律顧問／王秀哲・董安丹律師
著作權所有　翻印必究　Printed in Taiwan
ISBN 957-01-5661-9
YLib 遠流博識網　http://www.ylib.com　E-mail:ylib@ylib.com

Director/ Council for Cultural Affairs, Executive Yuan
Publishing institution/ National Center for Traditional Arts
Publisher/ Ko Chi-liang
Address/ No. 201, Sec. 2, Wubing Rd., Jisin Village, Wujie Township,
　　　　 Yilan County, Taiwan R.O.C.
Project director/ Fang Chi-shu, Chen Jin-chuan
Project staff/ Huang Su-chen, Chiu Jian-fa, Lin Jian-hua
Tel/ (03) 960-5230　Fax/ (03) 960-5237

Editing and production work/ Division of Books on Taiwan,
　　　　　　　　　　　　　　 Yuan-Liou Publishing Co., Ltd.
Address/ 6F, No. 81, Sec. 2, Nanchang Rd., Taipei 100, Taiwan R.O.C.
Tel/ (02) 2392-6899　Fax/ (02) 2392-6658　Postal account/ 0189456-1
Printer/ Innovation Graphic Arts Co., Ltd

Supervision/ Wang Chi-yong, Lu Chui-kuan, Lin Huei-cheng,
　　　　　　　Chiang Shao-ying
Text/ Cheng Hsi-ho, Cheng Chao-min, Chen Yi-fang, Chao Chi-fang
Translation/ Cheng Ming-hua
Case Photographer/ Kuo Chuan-chiu
Photographs by the courtesy of/
　　　　　 Yuan-Liou, National Center for Traditional Arts, Kaohsiung
　　　　　 Museum of History, Liao Tai Ji Photo Studio, Yang Ya-tang

Editor-in-chief/ Michelle Wang
Executive editor/ Wu Mei-ying
Layout editor/ Ann Kuo
Layout director/ Huang Kun-mou

Copyright advisor/ Attorney Hsiao Hsiung-lin
Legal advisors/ Attorneys Wang Hsiu-chih, Tung An-tan

國家圖書館出版品預行編目資料

台灣傳統藝術之美／鄭溪和等撰文：郭娟秋專
案攝影. – 初版. – 宜蘭縣五結鄉：傳藝
中心, 2003[民92]
　　面：　公分

ISBN 957-01-5661-9（精裝）

1.民俗藝術－台灣－照片集　2.工藝－文
化－台灣－照片集

673.24024　　　　　　　　　　92021132

台灣傳統藝術之美／鄭溪和等撰文：郭娟秋專
案攝影. – 初版. – 宜蘭縣五結鄉：傳藝
中心, 2003[民92]
　　面：　公分